8:15

A True Story of Survival and Forgiveness from Hiroshima

DR. AKIKO MIKAMO

Copyright © 2019 by Dr. Akiko Mikamo.

All rights reserved. No part of this publication may be reproduced, distributed, or transmitted in any form or by any means, including photocopying, recording, or other electronic or mechanical methods, without the prior written permission of the author, except in the case of brief quotations embodied in critical reviews and certain other noncommercial uses permitted by copyright law.

Photography by Andrew J. Flores and others (Credits in Appendix A)
Title Page Image by Eclair Bell
Map graphics by Uz Inc.

Printed in the United States of America.

Library of Congress Control Number: 2013912182

ISBN	Paperback	979-8-88887-324-3
	Hardback	978-1-64361-989-7
	eBook	978-1-64361-988-0

Westwood Books Publishing LLC
11416 SW Aventino Drive
Port Saint Lucie, FL 34987

www.westwoodbookspublishing.com

CONTENTS

Dedication v
Acknowledgment vii
Chapter 1:   Blue Sky, Red Sky 1
Chapter 2:   The River 18
Chapter 3:   The Day After 23
Chapter 4:   Demons 32
Chapter 5:   Miso Soup 40
Chapter 6:   Teruo 49
Chapter 7:   Separation 57
Chapter 8:   Goddess 63
Chapter 9:   Euthanasia 75
Chapter 10:   Being a Man 82
Chapter 11:   Postcard 91
Chapter 12:   Discharge 98
Chapter 13:   Okayama 107
Chapter 14:   Pocket Watch 113
Chapter 15:   Miyoko 118
Chapter 16:   The Last Family Member 126
Chapter 17:   Legacies 138
Afterword 165
Appendix A: Photos and Maps .172
Appendix B: President Barack Obama's Hiroshima Speech 193
About the Author 199

DEDICATION

This book is dedicated to my parents, Mr. Shinji Mikamo and Mrs. Miyoko Mikamo, and my beautiful children, Seira and Andrew.

ACKNOWLEDGMENT

First, I would like to thank my father, Mr. Shinji Mikamo, and my late mother, Mrs. Miyoko Mikamo, for having amazing human strength and resilience to survive the Hiroshima atomic bomb explosion, create their family life out of the ashes, and bring me and my sisters into this world. They also taught me the importance of forgiveness and having empathy for others, especially for those who have different backgrounds, beliefs, and values. They dedicated their whole life to raising, educating, and guiding us, not so much for their own family prosperity, but more for the humanity.

I would also like to express my deep gratitude to all my mentors, professors, and colleagues, who helped me learn about humanity and supported me throughout my personal and professional development, including but not limited to: Prince Nawab Mir Mohsin Ali Khan, Councillor Frances Stainton, Ms. Shirley Beljon, Dr. Mikihachiro Tatara, Dr. Katsuhiko Takahashi, Prof. Peter Kuznick, Dr. Neil Ribner, Mr. Ikunosuke "Mike" Kawamura, Dr. Michael Lardon, Dr. Lisa Bryce, Dr. Patricia Heras, Mrs. Kaoru Ninomiya, all my professors and colleagues at INSEAD and California School of Professional Psychology at Alliant International University, and many others.

I couldn't have completed the original project without tremendous help from my editor, Ms. Billie Fitzpatrick, who took deep interests in the subject and guided me all the way since my first draft. Thank you so much.

My family is the essence for my living force, and my children, Seira Mikamo Flores and Andrew J. Flores, taught me important lessons of life more than anybody else by being who they are. They also supported me 100% for this book project. They have also taken active parts in our Non-Profit Organization, San Diego-WISH's peace and humanity promotion. My sisters, Dr. Keiko Shintaku and Ms. Sanae Mikamo, and my extended family members also all gave me unconditional love and support.

I thank all my patients, clients, students, readers, and audience for giving me the opportunities to help in some ways and grow together.

Akiko Mikamo, PsyD, MP, EMCCC
San Diego, California, USA

I am **Shinji Mikamo**.

I am 19.

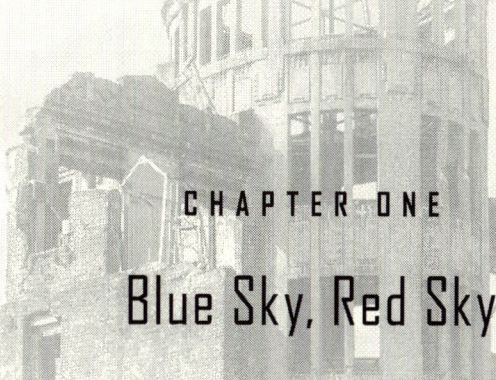

CHAPTER ONE

Blue Sky, Red Sky

Hiroshima, Monday, August 6, 1945

THERE WERE MANY THINGS about this morning that were just like any other. My father woke me around 7 a.m. We ate our breakfast at our small kitchen table, our legs crossed beneath us on the floor. We ate a meal that had become typical for us, in those food-rationed wartime days: millet and barnyard grass porridge. Over the past several years, as Japan had moved from war with China to the war in the Pacific against the U.S. and Allied forces, food and essential supplies of all kinds had grown increasingly scarce. Rice was heavily rationed and had almost entirely disappeared from our diet. Sugar and sweet fruits had completely stopped coming in from Southeast Asia. Supply lines to and from Japan had been seriously disrupted, as our nation's enemies routinely sunk our cargo ships. It seemed we'd been at war forever and that we would always be at war.

Our government had for years been waging a tenacious campaign to mobilize the spirit of Japan's entire people in support of the war effort. *"Doing Without Until Victory! Waste Is The Enemy!"* These slogans and rallying cries did nothing to quell my hunger, or to make the thin gruel in our bowls that morning taste better.

1

My father applied his typical sarcasm and razor-sharp humor to our difficult circumstances. I once heard him say to a neighbor about our food-rationed lives: "Well, I wake up early nowadays because I'm being fed bird food." This was always followed by a stretch of his throaty laughter.

The sun was not yet high, but already a sign of the hot pall of August engulfed us. Hiroshima in summer was suffocating. The tufts of air that wafted through the red clay walls over the bamboo frames and wood and paper doors mocked us. We knew that in a very short time, the temperature and humidity would be oppressive.

This morning, we did not move into our day with our usual discipline. Instead, we lingered, in a shared but unspoken hesitation. For there was something about this particular morning that was far from typical. Today was the day my father and I would finish preparations for the demolition of our home.

Many months of air raids by enemy forces in cities across Japan had caused tremendous damage, with millions dead and whole swaths of cities destroyed by fire. The relentless bombing and its destruction had led the Japanese government to issue building evacuation orders in Hiroshima and other cities throughout the country.

The government demanded the demolition of homes to help control fire in the event of an air-raid bombing. The authorities believed that demolishing the paper and wood houses that flourished throughout the crowded streets of Hiroshima would help to prevent a fire from rapidly spreading if, like most other cities, we were bombed by the Americans. Air raid drills that rang out at all hours of the night throughout the city were a constant reminder that it was less a question of if, than when.

Our family home was located in a demolition zone. We were to pick up whatever we could gather in the house and prepare for the structure to be torn down. Dozens of homes in our section of the city were being demolished in the same way. Our government did not concern itself with where we would go, once our houses had been destroyed. That was left to us to figure out. Fortunately, a family in our neighborhood had provided us with a place to stay. The Tanakas, who lived nearby and whose property had been spared demolition, had a small guest house that they had offered to us. We felt badly about imposing on the Tanakas. And yet we had no choice but to accept. We were not allowed to leave the city. Only elementary school-aged children and sick people were allowed to move to the countryside with government-issued permits.

Amid the frustration and anger of losing our home, we considered ourselves fortunate to have a place to go, and kind neighbors willing to help. I knew this was because of the great respect that the Tanakas, like so many people in our neighborhood, had for my father.

My father and I had worked long hours the previous day to complete the work preparing our house for demolition. But we hadn't finished. So, instead of going to my civilian job with the army the next morning, I stayed home so we could finish the last of the labor. I did not want to miss work. I was very reluctant to ask for the day off, and walked nervously, in the Sunday evening darkness, to my superior's office to make the request. I had no choice. At 63, my father was too old to manage the preparations for the demolition of our house on his own.

Like so much else related to the long, drawn-out war, these evacuation and demolition orders didn't make much sense. My father and I found the government's plan to be baffling and misguided. We grumbled about it as we finished our morning soup. "It makes no sense," growled my father.

I'd seen first-hand the destruction that the enemy air raids could do. It was just a few months before, in late May, when I had traveled through Tokyo. I was making my way back to Hiroshima from Sendai, a city located to the north, where I had stayed for a month to work as a trainer at their new armory. I passed through the capital city on the day after Tokyo had been bombed. That May 24 bombing was Tokyo's fourth major air raid since March. Other cities had been bombed as well, but nowhere had been hit worse than Tokyo. Our capital city had been subjected to more than 100 air raids. On March 9, 1945, hundreds of B-29s carpeted the city with bombs from 11 o'clock in the evening, through the long night until dawn. When the raid was over and the damage tallied, more than 100,000 people had died and half the city was destroyed. Even though many of the very young and very old had been relocated to the provinces, many women, small children, and adolescents were killed. Others remained in underground encampments, living like gutter rats with very little food and water every time there was an air raid.

It was pitch dark as my train approached Tokyo from the north. Then, with still two hours to travel before we reached the city, we saw the red night sky hanging over Tokyo, aglow with fire from the bombs. The sun rose before we arrived in Tokyo. Residual flames and smoke were everywhere. Most of the buildings were burned into ash and rubble.

This was why my father and I knew that these demolition orders were ridiculous. How could the government not realize the purposelessness and futility of demolishing houses in Hiroshima? Having seen the fierce power of those bombs, I knew there was nothing that would prevent destruction if our city were raided by a fleet of B-29s carpeting the sky with bombs.

Despite our profound regard for our Living God, Emperor Hirohito, my father and I had begun to lose faith in the Japanese government's policies and procedures. The demolition orders seemed absurd, and the austerity measures were tiresome.

We all wanted an ending to this prolonged war, believing that the ending could only come by winning. Though it seemed increasingly illogical, we were still being made to believe by our government and military leaders that some miracle would happen, and Japan would win the war in the Pacific. Our nation had a long and storied history of overcoming more powerful enemies. In 1905, during the Russo-Japan war, Japan overcame impossible odds to defeat Russia, a large and powerful country with military forces almost ten times the size of our own. Centuries earlier, when Mongolia had beaten and conquered China's Song Dynasty in 1281, and then tried to invade Japan, a big typhoon came with hurricane-like winds that prohibited the Mongolians from being able to maneuver their warships through the Sea of Japan. Thanks to these miraculous winds, Japan was able to successfully defend against the Mongolian invasion. These miraculous winds were later called kamikaze or God's wind. Our leaders told us we must continue to believe in the divine right of Japan to victory. They invoked those miraculous winds as inspiration. The Imperial Navy had named its suicide attack special forces Kamikaze, hoping for similar miracles to beat our latest, more powerful and more resourceful enemy.

I had a growing seedling of doubt in my unconscious mind about the likelihood that Japan would win this war. We were massively outnumbered in ships, soldiers, weapons, and munitions. We were overmatched in air power, and certainly in money. All civilians were expected to do their duty and had dedicated our nails, pots, and pans to the war effort. Even a high ranking Buddhist temple's big bell and a former Prime Minister's bronze statue had gone to the forge. Anything made of metal was to be melted and turned into munitions.

The Imperial Navy and Army government led by Admiral and Prime Minister, Honorable Hideki Tojo bombarded us constantly with its propaganda: *"The Americans are evil! The Japanese are winning! The Japanese took Singapore, the Philippines, Hong Kong, and more and more!"* These headlines in the newspaper and across the airwaves no longer resonated with me.

The seed that had sprouted my germ of doubt had been planted during my earlier days when I held an electrical apprenticeship at the army armory, prior to being transferred to my current job at the General

Second Army Headquarters. One of my responsibilities at the armory was repairing short-wave radios. All short-wave radios were prohibited. Broadcasts across short-wave frequencies can travel long distances, and the military did not want transmissions from other nations, especially enemy nations, reaching its citizens. If a civilian were caught listening to the short-wave radio, it would be confiscated, and the person would be jailed, or worse.

When infantrymen or government workers returned to Japan after an overseas stint, short-wave radios were confiscated at customs, or the radios were modified, so they wouldn't work for short-wave broadcasting used by the military. It was my job to modify and repair them.

One day in early 1945, a colleague and I were tinkering with a short-wave radio when suddenly it spat out the following:

(chuck, chuck, chuck, chuck… the sounds of many people in wooden getas walking on a busy street) a woman's voice in perfect Japanese:

"Hello, everybody in Japan! Do you know what these sounds are? They are the sounds of people walking on a busy street in Ginza (a major shopping and entertainment district) in Tokyo back in the days before the war started. Do you remember how life was enjoyable back then? Back then, you had chocolate in stores. The produce stores used to display plenty of sweet bananas, not a few rotten tangerines like now. Don't you miss them? Don't you miss the fun times back then? Don't you want to go back to those days? This broadcast is coming from a ship very close to you! It would be so much better if Japan stopped fighting, and we end the war. Why don't we go back to the peaceful time?"

This was a shocking surprise. My young army colleague and I were fascinated and excited. We listened to the broadcast repeatedly.

We also knew to keep it secret. If our superiors, or anyone at our post were to discover the enemy communiqué, we'd be arrested and charged with treason.

Later, I confided in my father about our illicit discovery. I told him in detail about the strange but true-sounding broadcast. Unlike me, my father was not the least bit surprised. The battles are approaching, he told me, so it made sense that the enemy would say things like this.

By this point in the war, even speaking English was banned. Our government had stopped allowing English to be taught in schools since it was the enemy language. I was so disappointed when I was about to enter middle school because I had been looking forward to starting my English lessons.

My renegade father did not stay silent. "Not learn English? That's the stupidest thing to prohibit students from learning English. If Japan wants to win this war against America, we need to learn English all the more. How are they planning to rule the enemy country after winning? We can't even talk to American POWs if we don't know English." he said. He believed in the power of Japan.

But my father was not rash. He was careful to say such comments only in our house. One never knew who might report you to a government official. We believed that most of our neighbors would have been loyal to us. But in wartime, you could never be sure who was listening and watching.

The risks of betraying the government, in word or deed, were grave. Any act of treason was matched with a death sentence. We sensed that the war was not going as the government wanted us to believe. But we kept all our doubts to ourselves. And there was no question that we would follow the government's orders about the demolition.

We continued to linger over our breakfast bowls as the sun rose higher in the sky. As if trying to summon the energy for the task ahead, my father picked up his pocket watch from the kitchen table. He often kept it there so he didn't need to go to the next room and look at the clock. I heard the familiar jingle of the house key that was chained to his watch and thought about the fact that, once we demolished the lovely house, the keys would no longer have a purpose.

At least it was just the two of us here to deal with this upheaval. The remaining members of our household were not with us. My elder brother, Takaji, was in the infantry somewhere in the Philippines. My mother was living in the country with my aunt. My mother was very ill from advanced cirrhosis and therefore had been permitted to travel out of the city.

When I was still small, it would have been quite unusual for me to have been allowed to stay alone with my father, without a woman in charge of caretaking the home. But it was wartime, and my father, in typical fashion, rewrote the rules: he would watch over me since my mother was sick. But he could not also care for her, so she was sent to live with relatives in the northeast in the country area, far away from Hiroshima.

This turned out to be a blessing.

After breakfast, I climbed up to our wooden roof. The roof was covered with clay tiles. Since the Tanakas' cottage did not have a lavatory, we had decided we would build one using the materials from our own house. One by one, I pried the thick clay tiles loose with my hammer.

My father worked below me on the ground, cleaning and picking things up in the backyard. At age 63, my father was slowing down. He could no longer work tirelessly for days at a time. At nineteen, I was young, and the more demanding labor was naturally assigned to me.

I gazed across our neighborhood, which was in the Kamiyanagi-cho section of Hiroshima City. Our section of Kamiyanagi-cho was quite beautiful. There was the Sentei Garden, full of seasonal flowers. There was the sparkling Kyobashi River, which flowed clear and powerful nearby. There was the elegant architecture of the houses that belong to the wealthy, such as those owned by the former Medical

8:15

Director of the Imperial Army Hospital and the former Executive Chief Editor of a large newspaper company.

We had moved to this wealthy part of the neighborhood only a few years before, soon after I had left school and started working as an apprentice electrical technician at the army armory. Because my father was a well-respected photographer and regarded as a wise and accomplished man, he had been invited to bring his family and live in a house that belonged to the Kake family. Their son's family used to live there, in the house adjacent to his parents, but they had moved out of the city when he was transferred to a new job. Mr. Kake was very old, and Mrs. Kake appreciated help from a wise man like my father to give her advice and help with their family affairs. We loved this fine house and enjoyed its special privileges, such as our own private bath and a field next to our house we used for growing vegetables like tomatoes, cucumbers, and potatoes.

When I was young, we lived in a poorer neighborhood of Kamiyanagi-cho. At the time, my father was a photographer working for a big studio. He took family portraits, and he also took yearbook photos for colleges and universities in Hiroshima. He used to bring home piles of photos and yearbook pages to work on them. When we were young, my brother Takaji and I loved to look at these photographs.

Then, when I was in the fourth grade, the studio where my father worked went bankrupt. Japan was starting the war against China, and even college students were being drafted into the military as officers. Colleges and universities could not keep making yearbooks, and families didn't want to take portraits without their father or son. My father was no longer able to earn sufficient money from just taking photos of neighbors and friends.

We had to accept scarcity and deprivation of all kinds. My brother and I were told we would have to give up school and go to work sooner than we'd hoped. I had been excited to continue on to high school after graduating from elementary school. Instead, because our family had very little money, my brother and I both completed a two-year higher elementary school and went to work at the age of 14. I was a good student, second to top in the whole class. Leaving school was disappointing, but we had no choice.

Even though he was poor, my father was admired and revered as an artist and a wise man. Everybody in our neighborhood called him Mr. Mikamo, as if he were a teacher or the village chief. Our family name, Mikamo, was unusual, meaning "beautiful and sweet." My father was confident and modest at the same time. He was also creative. He had a talent for finding solutions to other people's problems. In our section of Kamiyanagi-cho, my father, Fukuichi Mikamo, fixed everything from broken gadgets to our neighbors' secret family affairs.

It was only about 7:45 a.m., but I could feel it was going to be a hot day. There was not a single cloud in the sky. Sweat trickled down my face as I unhinged the tiles one by one with my hammer. I was looking forward to that evening, when I would meet my friend Teruo near Sakae Bridge and go for a swim in the river. Early that morning, everything was calm. The blue sky was beautiful. Under the sky, I could see some of the small hills situated on a beautiful delta that was surrounded by mountains, rivers, and the sea that made up Hiroshima. The city was crowded, with mostly flat houses, some two-story houses, and a few taller buildings. The city was filled with wooden houses like ours, some bigger, some smaller. The streets of shopping districts were thick with crowds, busy already on this hot summer morning. Both an academic city and a military center, Hiroshima had many schools and several army installations.

My neighbors below sounded cheerful as they splashed water in a small pot to cool down the soil to make the summer heat tolerable. They happily said good morning to each other and passersby. Unlike Tokyo and so many other Japanese cities including Osaka, Nagoya, and Kobe, Hiroshima had not been the target of air raids that had brought such devastation to those cities. Maybe we had been spared for a reason.

8:15

Perhaps our karma was better than those in other cities. I hoped so, and I hoped the good karma extended to keeping Takaji safe while he was fighting the war in the Philippines. I missed my brother terribly.

My thoughts were interrupted by my father yelling from below. "Shinji, stop daydreaming. It'll only get harder as the day goes on," my father said.

"Okay Father, I'll keep working," I said. I quickened my pace with the hammer. To me, my father was a man you did not want to disobey.

"Be done by 8:30 a.m. We don't need many roof tiles," my father said. "We have more moving to do." Our makeshift lavatory was going to be very small, maybe, six square feet at most.

"Yes sir," I replied.

My father went back to work in the yard, cleaning up and sorting things out. I thought of how far my father had come. He had left his home in a small village in the middle of the Chugoku Mountains in Okayama Prefecture at the age of sixteen. He didn't believe that he could make much of his life in a rural community, so he headed for Kyoto to pursue his passion for photography. His artistic talent had been obvious from a young age through his ability to write beautiful calligraphy, an art highly regarded in Japan. And his photographs of life in the city were equally as beautiful. When he was about thirty years old, he moved to Hiroshima although I never really knew why. He was always a free thinker, perhaps even a bit of a wanderer.

He did not marry until he was thirty-nine years old, which was considered quite old. Growing up, I hardly heard my father speak of his life pre-marriage in Kyoto and Hiroshima. But he would just say to me, my mother, and my older brother, Takaji, "I was poor back then, but happy. Now, I'm still poor and still happy. Ha, ha!" and he would start to laugh. This was a habit of his, to laugh at his situations, even the difficult ones. But he would stop there. My father did not talk much at all about his life before marriage, whether in Kyoto or Hiroshima.

My first mother, the mother who gave birth to me, was Chiyono. But the mother who raised me was not the mother who gave birth to me. My father married Chiyono, and they had two sons, my brother Takaji and me. When my brother and I were still very young, my mother became sick with tuberculosis. She died when I was two years old. I have no memory of her, only stories of her kind, caring heart, and her love for Takaji and me. The mother I remember is Nami, Chiyono's older sister, whom my father married when I was five.

It was nearly 8:15 a.m. I had made good progress, I thought, as I lifted my right arm and wiped the sweat of my right brow against it, turning my face to the right when…

FLASH

Suddenly I was facing a gigantic fireball. It was at least five times bigger and ten times brighter than the sun. It was hurtling directly towards me, a powerful flame that was a remarkable pale yellow, almost the color of white.

Then…

BOOM

The deafening noise came next. I was surrounded by the loudest thunder I had ever heard. It was the sound of the universe exploding. In that instant, I felt a searing pain that spread through my entire body. It was as if a bucket of boiling water had been dumped over my whole body and scoured my skin.

At the same time, I was thrown into a pit of absolute darkness. What had happened? I couldn't see anything. I was in total shock. I could feel nothing at all.

I finally became aware that I was buried beneath pieces of wood and poles and beams from the collapsed structure. Miraculously the only part of me that was not covered by debris was my head.

I had lost all sense of time and place. Was this real or just a bad nightmare? Was I still alive? I couldn't move.

Some of the thick dust began to settle, and my eyes began to adjust. It was dark, and I could only see out of my left eye. I felt panic rising in my throat. Had my right eye ruptured? I reached my hand to my head and felt the space over my eye. I realized I was bleeding heavily from my forehead. I felt around me, trying to get my bearings. I wondered if I was still in my house, or if I'd been thrown somewhere else. Everything had collapsed. Fragments of broken glass and china, charred clothes, wooden beams and shredded furniture were everywhere.

I could not see or hear anyone nearby. With my one good eye, I could only see a few feet in front of me. I was trapped under so much debris that I could not move. Even if I hadn't been buried by debris, I wasn't sure I could get up and move. I felt lightheaded and weak.

Then I heard my father shouting, "Shinji! Shinji! Where are you?"

I screamed for him at the top of my lungs. "Father over here! I can't get out!" My voice sounded cracked and broken, alien to my own ears. I could hear him making his way closer to me, crunching through the rubble.

At last he reached me. I was still completely covered with debris, unable to move. He tried furiously to pull me from under the weight of the debris. "We must get out of here," he said.

For the next few minutes, we struggled to move, desperate to get out from under the ruins of our home. The whole house had collapsed around us.

With a remarkable surge of strength, my father managed to move the heavy poles and beams that were pressing down upon me. I barely managed to move my body through the piercing maze of glass and splintered wood that covered me.

My face felt immobilized. I could barely see. Throughout my body I felt a terrible burning. I could smell the singeing of flesh burned raw.

I felt stinging heat on my leg. I looked down and saw my pants on fire. At that moment, my father tackled me and put out the flame that was surging up my leg.

My whole chest and right arm were completely burned. Horrible hot sensations covered my thighs. My skin hung of my body in pieces like ragged clothes. I looked down with my one good eye at my hands, my legs, and my belly. The raw flesh on my arms looked like a sweet yellow-powder cake my mother used to make before the wartime. I used to dream of this cake, I had longed for it so. Strangely, my skin in this condition looked beautiful. For just an instant, I felt calm. Then the reality of my situation hit me.

"Father, I can't see out of my right eye," I said, panic rising again.

My father took my face in his hands and examined me closely. "It's okay," he said. "You still have an eyeball. It's the blood coming down from your forehead that's covering your right eye." It was then that the screams began to assault us. From every direction, we heard human voices straining in pain, fear, and despair. People were shrieking for help all around us. These horrible sounds left us speechless. My father and I looked at each other, frozen.

We needed to move. I could barely walk. My father put his arm under and around me, supporting me as we took our first steps out of the rubble. The air was dark with ash and smoke, making it difficult to see. As my good eye adjusted to the semi-darkness, I froze at the sight in front of me. Everything had collapsed. In all directions, buildings were demolished, electric poles had fallen, trees had snapped and burned. Like ours, all of our neighbors' homes were destroyed, and probably them within. The only things that managed to stay standing were some steel frames of a few buildings.

It seemed as though Hiroshima had been turned into a gigantic pit of ash and rubble as far as the eye could see.

What in the world had happened? Had the sun exploded? I wanted to vomit.

8:15

My father remained calm.

"Bombs. They finally dropped them over us. They have demolished all of the houses for us. Roof. Tiles. Everything," my father said. He offered this explanation plainly, without dramatics or hysterics.

"I guess they saved us some labor," he added. Then he laughed out loud.

But I wasn't laughing.

All I wanted was to escape from this hell. I looked around desperately for some sign of life, some sign of normalcy or safety. A safe place where we could find shelter, food, water. There was none. There was only destruction, smoke, and fire.

"Shinji, we have to get out of here. We have to hurry." My father was mobilizing into action. He said he knew where we should go. First though, he explained, we needed to find our emergency backpack. Even in the middle of complete chaos my father remained calm.

I mumbled an okay. I couldn't help him search because of my injuries. I watched as my father rifled through the remnants of our home for our emergency supplies. He lifted broken furniture, moved fractured wooden poles, and sifted as best he could through the piles of debris.

At that moment I did not believe our situation could be any worse. Then we heard a roaring sound growing louder – a fire quickly approaching. We smelled and heard the fire before we saw it: an enormous conflagration of flame was leaping toward us.

My father stared hard at the flames. I could see him struggling to remain calm.

"Where is it? Where is the damn backpack?!"

The fire was drawing menacingly close. As it moved, it was burning everything in its path, anything that hadn't already been burned to ash in the explosion, including people. We heard their screams as the fire caught up with them. We smelled their flesh as they burned. We tasted the ash on our tongues.

It was hell on earth.

"We can't stay here any longer, Shinji. We must run NOW," my father urgently called to me.

My head was spinning in fear. I had no idea where and how we could ever escape, but my father seemed to have a plan.

"Sakae Bridge," he said and grabbed my hand. Sakae Bridge was the nearest bridge to us. A structure of concrete and steel, if anything nearby had withstood the explosion, and might offer some protection or escape, it would be the bridge.

Our house was only ninety yards away from the bridge, but it took forever to get there. Our vision was limited by the thick cloud of dust and ash that permeated the air. And I still could not see out of my right eye, as my head continued to bleed. As we fled the large flames that threatened us from a distance, we still had to dodge smaller fires that blazed all around us. We crawled under electric wires and fallen poles and stepped on the sharp and jagged debris. My bare feet were raw. So was the right side of my upper body. My entire body was in pain. Pain, however, was not my concern, nor was it my father's. We had to get to Sakae Bridge or we'd be consumed by the monstrous fire heading our way.

Around us, our neighbors were also trying to escape, dragging their wounded bodies forward in desperate, chaotic attempts to save themselves. One man not much younger than my father carried an elderly woman on his back. She was bathed in blood, with jagged pieces of glass stuck all over her back. More people who were gravely wounded were draped on the backs of others, who struggled to carry them to some safe place.

I heard whispers and cries from the ground. "Help. Help." "Water…"

Amidst the cries of suffering, I could also hear courageous words of encouragement, as those people who could still stand urged others to keep going.

We finally reached the Sakae Bridge. It was still standing. A crowd of perhaps a hundred had already gathered, and hundreds more were streaming toward the bridge and the river.

I tried to open my eyes wide to count the people. Wherever I looked, there were men and women covered with horrible, disfiguring burns. I couldn't count. I turned my head away, unable to look at the carnage. But it was impossible to escape. At every turn there were wounded people surrounding us, screaming and bleeding and grasping at survival. I could barely see out of my one good eye. But it didn't matter. The masses of burning bodies filled my vision.

"What's happening?" I said to my father.

He just shook his head and said, "We are going there." He pointed toward a crowd gathering on the left bank of the river. We made it to an empty spot on the left bank, behind the Sentei Garden. We were able to sit down under a tree in the shade.

But our respite only lasted a few minutes. The next thing we knew, someone screamed, "Fire! Fire is coming. Get into the river."

My father helped me stand up. I was too weak to do it on my own. He held tightly to my left arm, the only part of my body that was not burned. We inched our way to the river about ten feet away. With each inch, I felt like my whole body itself was made of steel, heavy and unwilling to move. With the help of my father, I forced myself to get into the water. I had no skin left, but I wasn't even feeling pain anymore. I had just become numb.

CHAPTER TWO

The River

THE ENORMOUS FIRE ACROSS the river in the section of the city called Osuga-cho was swallowing everything in its path. It had become a giant snake of fire, slithering through the streets. Fierce charcoal-color plumes of smoke filled the sky. Their dark, swirling columns and the leaping, angry flames reflected on the river's surface. Black smoke and red fire on the water. Red and black. Hell painted with merely two colors.

The Kyobashi River was at full tide. Even near the shore, the water was more than three feet high. Hundreds, perhaps thousands of people had fled to the riverbank and were now throwing themselves into the river, seeking refuge from the fire and, for many, relief from their third-degree burns. Already, bodies were floating, face down.

The current was weak. Normally, it would be nothing to stand in that quiet flow of river. Weakened by our injuries and surrounded by panic on all sides, we had to fight just to stay standing. We struggled not to be shoved or tossed or pulled under the water by the chaos of struggle that surrounded us. My father and I clung to each other. We used all our meager strength to stay above the water.

Many could not. All around us, people were collapsing in the crowded water, now churning from the desperate movement of hundreds of frantic souls. Many of those who collapsed were elderly.

8:15

Others had injuries so grave that they could do nothing but sink into the water. One after another, we watched people drop and begin to float away, joining the scores of other bodies. Those of us who were managing to stay upright could do nothing. We wanted to grab them, to rescue them. But most of us were not strong enough ourselves. We had no choice but to watch in agony as others floated down the river to their death.

I wanted to help these poor strangers. I wanted to reach out, to save even one. I did not have the strength. I was relying on my father's strength to help me stay upright.

"I'm sorry. I'm so sorry," I cried out to the stream of bodies as they floated by.

"Please forgive me that I can't help," I murmured my apology over and over again. My father squeezed my arm.

"Worry about yourself. It is all you can do," he said quietly.

I knew he was right.

I don't know how long we stood in the water. It felt like an hour, but it could have been ten minutes. At some point, I became aware of the throbbing pain in my body. The fire loomed at us from across the river, but it did not encroach upon the water. After a time, my father and I crawled onto the riverbank, the remains of our clothes soaking wet and dripping.

The scene that surrounded us was one of chaos, pain, and hysteria. Nearby, an innocent baby was suckling on his mother's breast as if nothing had happened, while she lay still on the ground, practically naked, her body covered in charcoal burns. An elderly man lay on his stomach. His back, swollen with deep burns, looked like a hippo. He was unable to move.

A woman stood alone in the crowd. Her hair stood straight on end. She gazed around with a vacant stare, looking like a ghost. She was yelling hysterically.

"I couldn't. I couldn't save my child," she wailed. "The fire came so fast. I had to leave my child behind. I killed her!" Her cries were chilling.

A new kind of panic crossed her face. "Oh no," the woman screamed. "I have to go to City Hall tomorrow to report my child's death officially. I don't know how I could make it to City Hall, I can hardly walk! I'll be in big trouble!" She did not grasp the abolishment of City Hall. Even amidst the destruction and agony, we remained, if only in our minds, in the tight grip of our government and its bureaucracy.

I could tell my father wanted to offer her words of comfort. But he said nothing and looked away. What words were there to comfort a mother who had lost her child this way? This was grief no words could console.

My ears picked up the confused chatter as others began to talk about what had happened. People escaped from Ebisu-cho, Kanaya-cho, from every neighborhood in Hiroshima to converge at the riverbank. Everybody thought that only their section of the city was bombed. I overheard someone say, "I thought it wouldn't be bombed over here, and that's why we came." It dawned on me that the whole city had been bombed. At that moment, an overwhelming feeling of sunken despair came over me as I realized that nothing could be worse than our current reality.

But I was about to discover I was wrong.

Across the river, dark clouds were descending strangely low in the sky. They looked like great thunderclouds. The cloud began to swirl, picking up speed and rousing thick ribbons of dust from the ground below. The twirling cloud began to stretch toward the sky. The tornado climbed nearly 60 feet toward the heavens, while visiting new destruction on the ground. It sucked up large pieces of collapsed houses, burned remains of furniture, and even water from the river.

This dark monster was dashing its way toward us.

All of us on the far shore of the river dropped to the ground, making ourselves as flat as we could. People grabbed whatever was in reach. Some clung to trees. Some clung to each other. The funnel cloud rained on us with debris.

People screamed for help. Their voices were lost, swallowed by the deafening noise of the tornado. Next to me on the ground, my father pressed my hand as we lay low and still. I was so petrified that I was holding my breath. There was no way we could withstand against this encroaching dragon.

Then the twirling beast hit the riverbank right in front of us. The dark tunnel of wind and debris shifted its direction and began to move towards the upper river. We had been spared. I took a gulping breath and felt my father's hand relax above my own.

I don't know how long we were sitting on the ground soullessly. I felt something wet and muddy on my left hand. A black smudge. Then, another one on my burned thigh, then a few more. Before I knew, black rain like liquid charcoal from the sky smeared my head, face, and all over my body.

By sunset, the huge fire and tornado had settled down. It seemed these twin monsters had gobbled every bit of the city that the bomb itself hadn't completely destroyed. Hiroshima, it seemed, was now a complete ruin.

As night fell, my father and I left the tree where we had found shelter and began moving slowly toward the Sentei Garden. I don't know why we moved. Others were going, and my father and I joined the stream of the wounded, dragging our heavy heads and nearly destroyed bodies toward the garden a couple hundred yards away. We moved slowly, our bodies seizing in pain, our feet shredded by debris.

We arrived at Sentei Garden at night. Only yesterday bursting with the colors of summer bloom, this beautiful garden was now gritty and black from the blast. Trees had been thrown to the sky by the tornado and dropped, broken and lifeless.

The garden was crowded with people. My father and I found a small space of ground to lie down. I was exhausted, but I could not sleep, even for a moment. Every nerve in my body felt lit with painful fire. I turned to my father next to me.

"Father, what's going to become of us now?"

My father did not respond. We uttered no more words that night. We just lay there in the darkness. That night there was not a single star. It was as if we were in a long pitch-black tunnel, the two of us side by side. I could see no light at the tunnel's end, only more darkness.

It was by far the longest night of my life.

CHAPTER THREE
The Day After

AT DAWN THE NEXT day, those who could move began roaming the garden and beyond, into different sections of the city.

My father and I hadn't slept at all. Several times during the night, my father rose from the ground and went to the river, returning with handfuls of water for me to drink. My scorched skin had made me unbearably thirsty.

We were in a haze, much like the smoldering surrounding us. A man nearby told us that the military was treating the injured at the East Army Drill Ground, to the east.

My father and I decided to go there. We hoped to find medical help. We also wondered if we might encounter neighbors and friends there. We had hope that we could find that some others we knew had survived the blast and its aftermath.

Apparently, many others had the same idea. We joined a steady stream of people walking in the direction of the drill ground, which was located behind the Hiroshima Train Station.

Once again, we had to come back to the Sakae Bridge. That morning we retraced some of our steps from the day before. We revisited the previous day's horrors, and we encountered new anguish.

The bridge was covered with people. Many of the badly burnt people were lying on their stomachs. It looked as if they'd been dropped from above. Many were dead. Some were alive. Others were lingering precariously in between.

As we were about to cross the bridge, my father hesitated. "So many people," he sighed. "Can we walk through?"

I wondered the same thing myself. There was hardly any room to put our feet down, so inundated was the bridge with fallen people. We traversed slowly, doing our best to step around the many lifeless bodies in our path.

My feet were charred and clumsy. Every step or so, I would unintentionally hit an arm or a leg and hear the person below me wince in pain. I felt like a vulture. Crossing that bridge, and leaving all those wounded people behind to die. But I couldn't stop because I was in so much pain. It took every ounce of my energy to put one foot in front of the other. The soles of my feet were intensely sore. Like so much of my body, they had hardly any skin to protect them.

In front of me I saw a pair of women's geta, wooden slippers left all by themselves. Without thinking, I started to put them on my aching bare feet. A woman lying down nearby moved her fingers slightly toward me.

"Mine," she breathed out in a low tone.

My hand recoiled from the slippers. Horrified, I placed the woman's slippers together and put them at her fingers' reach.

"So sorry. I didn't know," I murmured.

I was afraid she would never be able to wear those wooden slippers. I knew she was dying. Repelled by my act of mindlessness, I hung my head as I moved away from her, her near-lifeless fingers just beyond the reach of the slippers.

At the far end of the bridge, I saw a charcoaled body of a young boy. His skin looked as if it would slide off if you touched him. His body was like a charred piece of kindling left in the fireplace. Decades later, I still wondered if this was our neighbor's boy, whom they never found.

8:15

Slowly, with my heart breaking into countless pieces, I stumbled forward. I did my best to follow exactly in my father's footsteps, hoping and believing he would know the path to save us both.

At last we arrived at the East Army Drill Ground, an open field of overgrown grass, a little more than a half-mile square. A depressing wire fence bordered the periphery. At one time this land had been used as fields for growing rice and vegetables. The military had appropriated the land in 1890 to use for exercises and drills.

It was a familiar place to me. As a young child, I'd played in the wild grasses of the field. My friends and I had spent many hours here playing freely under the sun's pleasant rays. We flew colorful kites held aloft by warm breezes. We caught bugs of all kinds in our cupped hands, chirping crickets and elegant grasshoppers. We chased dragonflies, grabbing after their iridescent wings. I recalled one afternoon when, in my childish determination to run faster and catch a bobbing dragonfly in flight, I slipped out of my geta, leaving them behind in the tall grass as I ran. I caught that dragonfly but lost my slippers. I remembered my friend and I combing through the reedy stalks of grass, searching. I could not go home without my slippers. We were tired, hot, and thirsty when we found them, but relieved at escaping the prospect of facing my father's fury. These childish games and worries were now from another lifetime, another world.

When I grew older, I went to work for the civilian corps of the army. Recently, they had me working in the Onaga Elementary School, which stood at one edge of the drill ground. I saw this field almost every day, empty and largely unused. Now it was crowded with people milling around. Many could not stand, and were crawling instead of walking. With so many wounded people, I wondered if we would be able to get any help. Several lines were forming, toward what seemed to be a medical station.

We put ourselves at the back of one line, my father behind me. My father said nothing as we sat cooking in the scorching heat. The blazing sun was baking my skinless body. Hundreds of people were ahead of us in line. Soon it seemed that there were as many behind us as well, as people poured into the drill ground seeking shelter and care.

I could barely move, but I craned my neck as best I could, trying to see to the front of the line. I was looking for a white medical tent, or any sign of something that looked official, a promise of real help. I saw no such things. The only thing I could see were wounded people in front of me, behind me, and swarming across the sweltering hot drill ground. The open field had no trees or anything else to provide respite from the merciless sun.

We waited endlessly in line, inching forward every so often. Like most people, we could not stand. We lay on the ground and crawled our way forward. I watched as many people sank to the ground and became stuck, as if glued there. They were too weak even to crawl. Collapsed, these people faded into death before ever having the chance to receive help.

That's what's going to happen to me, too. I thought as my father and I panted and waited under the unforgiving blistering heat. The sun was hot, and the heat only made our circumstances that much more unbearable, but even worse was the added pain it caused. So much of my body had been peeled of skin, and the sun burned into my raw flesh. I felt as if I were being stabbed by balls of thick needles, over and over.

I couldn't stop thinking of water. Water dribbling on my tongue, down my throat, cooling my skin. Water. I so badly wished somebody would give me water or just some old newspaper for just a bit of shade. I was not alone in my desperate thirst. Everyone around us was begging for water, or anything to ease their suffering.

At this point, I wasn't even afraid of dying. The pain was beyond imagination, and I just wanted to be free from it. I longed to feel the sensation of my own death. If I died, I wouldn't have to keep suffering.

8:15

My only wish was that my father would survive. This seemed likely since his wounds appeared less serious than mine.

As the hours passed, and we still waited, people around us grew increasingly desperate. My father and I listened to the pleas of people ahead of us and behind us in line. They plead to no one in particular.

"Please, please. Is it my turn? How much longer? Please take a look at my wounds. I'm going to die from the heat."

My father pushed me forward. "Keep going," he said simply. I listened. I tried to let the firm sound of his voice and his strong, calm demeanor quiet the sounds of those dying pleas that echoed in my head.

Finally, we reached the head of the line. There was no sign of refuge. No medical clinic, no hospital beds, no doctors, no antibiotics, no painkillers. Nothing. They were not even providing simple shade, something to block us from the sun. At the end of this long line there were only a few corpsmen who seemed overwhelmed. They seemed confused and bewildered by the task of providing even basic medical help.

I tried to turn around to look at my father, to find some direction or reassurance in his face, but my head couldn't move.

Instead I dragged my body toward a corpsman, who then sat me on the ground. Everything was swollen; my face, arms, legs. The corpsman, who probably knew as much about healing burns like these as I, gazed at me without emotion. He poured some kind of cleansing liquid over my burns. The cleanser stung like hell as it made contact with my scorched and raw skin. But I had no energy left to even move or to cry out. All I wanted was some water.

To my surprise, the simple treatment did make me feel a little bit better. It might have been because of the intense relief I felt at no longer having to wait. Whatever the source, this moment was the first tiny sliver of hope I had felt since the whole disaster had started.

I managed to turn around in my father's direction. I wanted to share this bit of hope with him.

"Father, I think I feel a little –"

I lost my words in the middle of my sentence.

My father was gone. I had assumed he had been behind me the whole time. I couldn't believe my eyes.

I started to scream. "Father, where are you?"

I felt my mind begin to shatter, overwhelmed with fear. A moment ago I could not move. Now, in my panic, I pulled myself up and started to walk.

I stumbled the length of the drill ground, from Kokuzen-ji Temple in the East to Tosho-gu Shrine at the West end, desperately seeking my father.

In those terrifying moments I forgot about my excruciating pain. I became like a young child lost in a busy street, hysterical to be reunited with my parent and protector.

"Father! Where are you? Father?" I screamed like a madman. Traversing the grounds was difficult. The field was filled with hundreds of dying people who begged me for water, who grabbed and clung to my ankles and my legs as I moved. I pulled their hands off my body and kept moving.

"I'm sorry," I said, again and again. My voice was feeble.

I could feel myself losing my sanity under the weight of the terror I felt at being separated from my father, at being alone. I began to shout words that were nonsensical. "No way. Alone. Totally alone now? From now on? This can't be real. No. No. No. Father, don't leave me. Please. Don't leave me. Where are you?"

There was no one to help. I was surrounded by strangers. People were from all over the city, and they did not know my father. There was no one to ask. I staggered, shouting like a lunatic screaming. I finally collapsed, taken down by the grim reality of my situation. I had lost my father. I wanted to die. I was envious of the dead.

I lay there for some time, willing myself to death. Then something happened. I felt a force deep within me. Perhaps it came from outside of me. Wherever it originated, I felt a power that I didn't know I had. It was a force separate from me and yet in complete control of me. I pushed myself back up. With my swollen face, exposed flesh and charcoaled leg, I once again dragged myself across the yard in search of my father. I don't know how long this went on. It could have been minutes, or an hour. I kept searching until I could not walk another step on my swollen bare feet. I was exhausted. I finally gave up once again. My energy drained out of my whole body, and I slid down to the ground along the side of a tree murmuring, "Father, where are you?"

I heard a voice calling my name. "Shinji, Shinji."

At first I did not believe my ears. Was that my father's voice?

I could not tell if I was hallucinating, or if I had conjured his voice from my terror and desperation, from my madness. Nothing seemed real anymore. I felt I was in a nightmare I would never wake from.

And then my eyes fell upon a familiar figure on the ground about ten feet away. It was my father. Really him.

"Where did you go?" I cried out as I crawled as fast as I could in his direction. My pain was forgotten. My energy surged. I reached my father and clung to him, bursting into tears.

"Father," I sobbed. "Why did you leave me alone? Please don't ever leave me again."

It was a miracle I had found him in this chaos, amongst so many people. I felt like I was going to be saved because I had found my father.

We lay side by side on the ground, and he told me what happened.

Unbeknownst to me, while waiting in line, he fainted. A policeman happened to walk by and found him passed out. The officer gave him a shot of some kind of medication. Then he carried my 63-year-old father quite a distance away to a shady tree so he could rest. It was there that my father came to realize he had lost me.

"I was so worried about you," I said, tears welling up in my eyes. I felt guilty. I should have noticed when he disappeared behind me. All I could think about while waiting in that line was getting help for my burns. We were lucky, so lucky. It was unbelievable to feel lucky on this day, in this place. But we did.

At this point, the sun was starting to set. I lay next to my father trying to fall asleep. As darkness fell, and all throughout the night, I heard people begging for water. So many of the wounded were too weak to get up from the ground and walk to a stream nearby. They lay in pain and thirst, unable to relieve either.

From the ground, the injured were grabbing the legs of anyone who walked by in the darkness, as they had done to me hours earlier. "Somebody… please give me some water." The groans and moans of these people clinging onto the last threads of life echoed around me all night, haunting me. Between all the strangers' moans and my fear of losing my father again, I could hardly sleep. "Father, Father," I said.

"I'm fine, Shinji," he replied in a tired voice. "Don't worry." Finally I dozed off, but only for a few minutes.

I woke with a start and checked to see that my father was still beside me. I repeated this over and over until the sun started to rise.

* * * * * * * *

"Morning?" I mumbled to myself. Two days of pain, panic, thirst, and exhaustion had left me confused. It was hard to know where I was, or whether it was day or night.

I called out to my father.

"I'm here, Shinji. Don't worry," he responded immediately. He knew how scared I was of losing him again.

"Please don't leave me again, Father," I begged him. I could not bear the thought of being separated, of experiencing that fear of being alone again. My father did not speak. He gently squeezed my hand.

It was his way, to communicate without words, with the simplest of gestures.

It was becoming more and more difficult to move my body. Once I lay down, I could hardly turn my head. I tried to look around by keeping my head still and moving my eyeballs. I felt my consciousness slipping away from me, and with it my sense of time and place.

I noticed a series of stone steps that looked familiar. I asked my father where we were.

"We're at the bottom of the steps of Tosho-gu Shrine." Being able to orient myself made me feel better. But that small relief lasted only for a moment. My father pointed to the shrine. "Shinji, we are going up," he shouted.

Had my father gone mad? I could hardly move. I knew he must be in pain as well. I did not understand why we couldn't stay and rest.

"Don't ask why. We are going," my father said authoritatively. "But Father, I can't," I replied. "I can't move."

"I'll help you," he said and extended his fragile arm for me to hold. It was the weak leading the weaker.

I did not understand why he wanted to go up to the Tosho-gu Shrine. Obviously he didn't feel like explaining his decision. There was no saying no. So as midday arrived, and with my father's help, I began to drag my heavy body up those familiar stone steps, one at a time.

CHAPTER FOUR

Demons

WE CLIMBED FIFTY STEPS to reach the top. We saw that a portion of the Tosho-gu Shrine had been destroyed by the blast. There were only a few people at the shrine, nothing like the chaos of the crowds at the drill ground below. We found shade at the back of the shrine. My father and I settled in a spot, lowering ourselves to the ground to rest.

I closed my eyes. For a moment, it felt like a peaceful Sunday afternoon, when my father and I would sit on the back porch and relax. But my pain was becoming worse with each passing moment. My skin, swollen and raw, my throbbing leg, my aching head and side, all reminded me that we were most certainly not relaxing on the back porch of my house.

It was Wednesday, August 8. Two days had passed since the bombing.

The day was hot and clear. We rested for a while in our spot behind the shrine. At around 3 o'clock my father made an announcement that shocked me.

"We are going back home to Kamiyanagi-cho," he declared.

I flew into a panic. There was nothing left for us at home. We had no home left at all. What could be the point of returning? My mother was in Okayama. My brother was off fighting the enemy. It was just my father and me. Finally, at the shrine, we had found some small measure of peace.

"Please, Father," I begged him. "Let's stay here."

"No questions," my father yelled back at me. "If we just stay here and do nothing we will only be waiting for death. There is no water. No food."

He moved to stand. "Get up now and follow me."

All I wanted was to be left in peace behind the shrine. I was ready to die. What was there to live for? Our life as we knew it was gone. My father, as though reading my thoughts, said, "Don't even think about giving up."

He drew his hands around my body and lifted me, helping me to stand.

To return to Kamiyanagi-cho we first had to descend from the shrine. It took enormous energy to start walking again. We stood at the top of another series of steps. I couldn't imagine making it down all those steps. My body felt heavy, and my burns unbearable. My body had stopped listening to me. I didn't want to move, not even one step forward. All I could think of was that I would rather sit down and die than make my way down this long trail of stairs. Once again, as though reading my mind, my father barked at me.

"Shinji! You are thinking bad thoughts, aren't you?" His scolding voice made me shiver.

I denied it. What else could I say to him? That I was ready for this hell to end, even if it meant my life with it? As the days and hours went by, my pain was only becoming worse. My wounds and burns were eating away at my body. I began to stagger down the long line of steps. My left leg was stronger than my right, so I brought that leg down one step, then paused. I pushed and dragged down my burnt right leg. Another pause. When I could summon the energy, I did it all again.

Three days ago, before the explosion, it would have been nothing to me to traverse these stairs. I would have skipped those stone steps two at a time, without a thought. But now, with my body decrepit, it took me more than a whole minute to go down one single step.

We had struggled to make it almost all the way down to the last 10 steps, when we encountered two Japanese soldiers. Both appeared to be in their early twenties. Each carried a sword and a gun. They stood below us on the steps like gatekeepers, blocking the rest of the stairway.

One shouted at us. "You can't go any further," the soldier yelled. He looked possessed.

"What?" my father said in disbelief. "This is the only way down."

"There's a slope on the other side of the shrine," said the other soldier. This second soldier pointed toward a steep dirt decline filled with brush and debris. We could see it was a tangled mess.

"That's impossible," shouted my father. He tried to reason with the two soldiers. He pointed out that we would have to walk to the top of the shrine before going down again over a terrain with no path. "Look at my son," my father said, "look at his wounds and burns. How in the world do you imagine he could go down such a slope?"

The soldiers hesitated for one moment. For just an instant it seemed possible that they might relent, that they would step back and allow us to pass. "Don't talk back," one called out angrily. "We have been ordered to guard this route. So there's no way we would let any single rat come down here." The soldier spat out his words with fury. While the other was speaking, the second soldier showed us similar rage in his demeanor.

My father was stunned. "Are you blind? Don't you see what's happening around here? What in the world could you guard when there's nothing left? To hell with your 'guarding' orders. Aren't you Japanese soldiers? Isn't it your duty to guard Japanese citizens?" my father ranted. He stopped only when one of the soldiers pointed his sword at my father's belt.

"Don't you want to savor your life?" he hissed at my father in a threatening voice. Then the soldier spat in my father's face. This was the ultimate act of disrespect. In Japan, the elderly were revered. To treat an elder this way was unthinkable. Were these demons wearing false justice as cover? Had the bomb changed everything? Had it destroyed not only our bodies, but our minds too?

In the many, long years of war, the military had come to be a constant presence in our lives. All of Japan's citizens were expected to honor and celebrate the nation's great army in all their words and deeds. Treason was constantly being sniffed out. The fear of being found to question the justness of war, the invincibility of our fighting force, was ever-present, and the consequences grave. We had been told that our military was all-powerful and all-capable, that winning was beyond question. To view these soldiers as thugs and murderers was the ultimate betrayal to the Empire.

My father was known for being fearless. If he had been alone on those steps, the soldier's threat would not have quieted him. He would have yelled expletives at these two awful young men even if it meant his death. His honor was at stake. That meant more to our culture than life itself. But with me by his side, my father held back. He withdrew from the soldiers' challenge in order to save me, to honor his duty as a father. If it hadn't been for me, my father would have never backed away from such injustice and disrespect.

Calmly, my father said, "We were the first to be up here. You came after us. It would be understandable if you wanted to stop people from climbing up. But it makes absolutely no sense to stop people from coming down."

"Shut up," they said in unison, like devils incarnate.

Clenching his teeth and holding his fists tight, my father turned to look at me. His gaze, so full of restrained emotion, almost looked through me.

"We are going up," he said.

"What? Again?" I said. I couldn't believe this.

"Just do as I say, Shinji," my father replied. "We are going up."

I thought of the labor and pain it had taken to travel down this far. The mere thought of enduring the additional pain just to retrace my steps was almost incapacitating. But I had no choice. I must listen to my father.

We turned and started up the steps towards where we started. I slowly dragged my body, which felt like it weighed a ton. The pain was unrelenting. But the humiliation and injustice we'd just experienced felt worse. My mind was spinning with questions. What was there to guard? Who gave those soldiers their orders? For what purpose? Where had they come from? Why weren't they there to help us? I knew there were no answers to be found. But I could not stop asking myself. Why, why had they been so pointlessly cruel?

I don't know how much time passed, how long it took us to retrace our steps. When at last we reached the top, all I could do was drag my swollen, battered body toward the side of the dirt slope, the one that we were now supposed to descend.

Behind us, a voice screamed out. "Go to hell, you old fart!" It was one of the soldiers below, yelling at my father. I could not believe my ears. My father did not even turn his head. He just said under his breath, "Dumbass. You have leisure time to watch us, but no time to help."

Father turned to me, and saw the look of shock and anger that was frozen on my face. "Forget it," he said. "Let's go."

He pulled my hand hard. I could tell he was holding in his anger.

We approached the side of the slope.

I knew this side of the slope beneath the Tosho-gu Shrine well.

As a child, I had come here with friends to play and pick chestnuts. As many as fifty to one hundred *torii* gateways had lined this narrow slope leading to the shrine. Torii are traditional Japanese gates that are often at the entrance to a Shinto shrine, either inside or outside. Passing under these soaring gates symbolizes the transition from the profane to the sacred.

8:15

My heart almost stopped when we finally reached the edge of the slope and looked down. Most of the dozens of Torii gateways had been shattered by the bomb blast. The long slope was covered with sharp and broken pieces of wood, rusted, menacing nails, tiny wooden prickles and huge splinters.

"No we can't go through here," I said to my father.

The slope was narrow, only a few feet wide. There was no side path to the left or the right. The sides were covered with broken shrapnel from the *torii* gateways. The only way down was to go through this jungle of piercing wooden splinters. These gateways that had once stood proudly crowning the path, ushering visitors to this tranquil and spiritual place, had been blown to pieces. Their remains now made up a hellish maze.

I did not think there was any way we could walk through this. But alas, there was no other way out. To help spare our feet and make walking easier, we did our best to move away the broken wood pieces with our hands. One by one, we picked up splintered shards of wood. Both my hands were monstrously swollen, and my arms were stiff and covered with burns. It was excruciatingly painful. Inch by inch, we moved through this non-existent path, my father and I over and over again being scraped and cut by these wooden remains that felt as razor sharp against my raw flesh as barbed wire.

I fumbled. "My body can't make it," I said to my father. I was almost crying.

"Move Shinji. Just move," he said, as he had so many times during these past two days. But this time, I heard meekness in his voice. He was wearing down, too. How could he not be?

I contemplated my choices for a moment, then made up my mind to keep moving. Crawling the whole distance, we inched downward, little by little. We traveled sixty-five yards, but it felt like half a mile.

Rage, resentment, pain, and agony all roiled inside me. It would have been easier if the Torii gateways had simply fallen down. Instead, the blast from the bomb broke down the gateways into a million prickles, thorns, splinters, and twigs. Every sharp point scraped my flesh. Perhaps if my skin had been there, the prickling and scraping might have been bearable. But so much of my body had lost its skin, and now pieces of my flesh fell off as if it were tattered pieces of clothing. The excruciating pain was consuming me. I felt as if sharp knives were scraping my body from the outside in. I was raw to the bone.

With every inch I moved, more of my flesh scraped off. I could not distinguish which parts of my body were hurting the most. All I could think was, *Goddamn this hurts. Hurts. Kills. I'm losing my mind. No more.*

Uncontrollable shrieks came out of my mouth with every scrape I endured. I could not bear this anymore. I pleaded with my father to stop. "I can't. I can't move another inch," I cried. "Please let me die. I would rather die and not feel this pain. PLEASE. I'm so thirsty I can't move. I don't want to move." I sat down with tears pouring from my eyes. I was desperate.

In the face of my desperation, my father stayed strong. He refused to allow me to give up. "You want to die? Don't say that word so lightly," he warned me. "We cannot turn back on the slope."

"At the bottom of the slope there is a stream," he reminded me. "You can quench your thirst there. I know you can do it, Shinji. No matter how painful it is, you are too young to die. You are not able to die at your age. As long as you stay alive, you will recover one day. The day will come. Just a bit more to go. Do it, Shinji," my father said.

He shouted these words to me over and over again as we made our descent. When I faltered, he physically pushed me forward. His forcefulness was a whip made of the toughest love. His yells were cheers. It worked, somehow. My father's constant pushing and shouting carried me down that beastly slope.

The whole time, with every painful step, I cursed those two soldiers and the senseless pain and suffering they had caused my father and me. Why did they punish innocent people already suffering in misery? What did we do to deserve that? For what sins were we being punished?

CHAPTER FIVE

Miso Soup

It took us two hours to reach the bottom of the slope. When we arrived, we encountered the stream my father had promised would be there. My lips and tongue were cracked and dry, my throat parched with thirst. I'd never experienced thirst like this, a thirst I could feel throughout my entire body. The sight of water was so heartening that it ever so slightly eased the sting of humiliation and anger I was feeling towards the soldiers from the Tosho-gu shrine.

Water.

As fast as my aching body would move, I dropped to the ground. My right hand was burned and useless, so I used my left hand to scoop water and bring it to my mouth. Over and over again I drank. My father did the same, kneeling beside me.

When my thirst was finally satisfied, I stood again. I looked around us. People lined the stream, sitting along its edge. They were not drinking, as my father and I had been. They were still. Clothes burned or missing altogether, skin scorched and bloody, so many wounded people sat staring into the distance. Shoulders slumped, spines curved in defeat. It was as if they were in a trance. They were alive, but it was as if their souls had already slipped away from their bodies.

In Buddhism, it is believed that to reach the afterlife, the dead must cross the Sanzu River, the River of Three Crossings. Some crossings are happy, as souls pass over a beautiful bridge decorated with jewels. But the Sanzu is also the crossing to the underworld, to darkness. Standing here, looking at these defeated souls, I felt as if we were facing the Sanzu itself, peering into hell.

Contemplating the afterlife, a thought came to me. If I just stopped breathing here by the water, I would be relieved from this pain. How liberating it would be just to let go, to be released from this broken body. In my mind, I felt a strong desire to surrender.

But my mind and body seemed to be at war with each other. My mind was ready to put an end to this living torture, to face the Sanzu River, wherever it might take me. But my body wanted to fight. As if it were a separate entity, and despite its incredible pain, the core of my physical being was somehow trying to stay alive.

I'm sorry, I whispered to my body. *I cannot go on any more.* I moved ever so slightly as if to sit down, to join those poor souls at the water's edge.

Then I looked up at my father.

He shot me a stern look in return.

"Don't slip into weakness so easily," he said sharply. "We've made it through the worst."

It was as if my father could read my mind. He knew my thoughts as well as I did. He sensed my weakness. He felt my temptation to surrender to pain and death. And he demanded instead that I be strong.

My father moved away from the water, heading in the direction of Sakae Bridge and our destination – home. I attempted to swallow my defeated thoughts. I breathed in deep and gathered all of my energy. With a will I did not know I possessed I propelled myself forward, following my father yet again.

As we headed toward the bridge and our old neighborhood, we saw new scenes of the destruction that had been bestowed upon our city. The streets were filled with people moving in all directions. Soldiers pushed a wagon filled with bodies of the dead piled one atop the other. People were combing through the wreckage, looking for things – food, supplies, anything at all – to salvage. The air was thick with a dust that made everything seem muddied and unreal. There was a deep sense of chaos.

We walked toward Osuga-cho, passing the ruins of the National Railway Hospital. The building was completely destroyed. No help to be found there. I saw smashed and melted medicine bottles, fused together to form large, misshapen masses of glass, the twisted remnants of bed frames, and precious first aid supplies undoubtedly ruined and lost. We saw what was left of the Hiroshima Railway Station, the massive terminal that housed several train lines that connected our port city to other cities across Japan. Huge sections of the building had collapsed. Steel beams that had once supported concrete walls now twisted free, bending misshapenly toward the ground. Parts of the station were somewhat intact, jagged walls of brick and concrete battered and crumbling but holding. Other parts had been completely destroyed. A fire burned in the distance, where a railway car had flipped its tracks.

Sakae Bridge was now just a few hundred yards ahead of us. With my father's constant encouragement, I forced myself to walk a few yards, then took a break. I had to lie down every few minutes and rest my aching, wounded body. My father was remarkably patient.

"I really can't walk any more. Can we just stay here for a while?" I withered to the ground. My mind was empty. My energy was drained. I could no longer command my legs to move.

But my father gave me no mercy. Every time I stopped and fell to the ground, he let me rest for a moment. Then he forced me to stand and move.

"The sun is setting. Get up, Shinji," he shouted.

His voice reached me in a place I couldn't reach myself. Every time he goaded me, I found a tiny sliver of energy I didn't think I possessed. Every time he ordered me, I stood up and staggered forward again.

8:15

Over and over, we replayed this scene, as we inched our way onward. It was a pace that must have frustrated my father, but I never saw his anger flare at me, or his impatience rise to the surface. I only saw his fierce spirit, his commitment to save both our lives.

We made it to Sakae Bridge at sunset. Hiroshima is a city of rivers. Our rivers had been clean and lovely. Now we stood at the Kyobashi River, which had once flowed clear and sparkling under the bridge. It was clogged with bodies, waterlogged and swollen, naked and burned, pushing against one another as they floated in water that had turned black as coal.

The wide expanse of the bridge, too, was covered with bodies, many dead, others dying still. Crossing seemed to take forever, as we tried desperately to step around the lifeless forms beneath us. It was impossible.

I slowed down, feeling my knees buckle beneath me.

"No. Don't stop," my father shouted. "We are almost home." Home? What home?

But my father continued to press me forward. "Almost there," he said, as we moved, inch by inch, between the decaying bodies.

We walked not just among the dead, but others like us, the barely living. Everywhere around us, people were struggling to move from one place to another. Burned and blackened by the explosion, hair sticking out in all directions, there were men, women, and children wandering all around us. Among these wanderers, I saw the same trance-like gaze I'd seen at the stream. Everyone was moving as if they were going someplace. But where? Where could any of us go? There was no escape. It felt as though we'd be wandering like this forever. We looked at each other hauntingly, knowing that in some other life, under some other circumstance, surely we would help one another. But no one had the strength. It was every man for himself. Were it not for my father, I would have died there.

Returning to what remained of Kamiyanagi-cho after the bomb was like visiting a foreign land. The familiar sights and markers of our lovely neighborhood were gone. The neat and tidy homes that lined our street had been reduced to piles of ash and rubble. My blistered and swollen feet never quite found the ground, so dense was the spread of rubble and ruin beneath us, littered across what had once been the place our family had lived so happily and comfortably.

In the quickly fading light of day, we slowly made our way through streets that had once been beautiful and well-tended. I saw burned shards of wooden beams and slats that had once made walls, broken bits of crockery and china. Piles of ash were everywhere. Trees shorn of leaves and branches stood, trunks burned to thin sticks. Every now and then we'd come upon a fragile post or half wall improbably still standing, looking lonesome and out of place amid the flattened remains.

This strange, flattened landscape stretched as far as we could see. As darkness began to fall, I could see spirals of smoke rising grey-white against the blackening sky, the remnants of the fires that had burned across the city.

My father walked in front of me, as I struggled to keep up. I couldn't imagine what we'd do when we arrived at the place where our house once stood. What was left for us there now? Would we even recognize our house when we found it?

Up ahead, a building came into view. A concrete structure that had withstood the assault of the bomb. I squinted, trying to determine where we were.

"The Shimazus' warehouse," my father said. The Shimazus lived next door to us. They had a storage building adjacent to their home. This was the building we were looking at now. We'd made it home, or at least to what was left of home.

By the time we reached the area where our house had stood, it was completely dark. My father walked amid the ruins of our lives, stopping to bend and sift through the rubble.

8:15

I thought of his photographs, his livelihood. Because my father was a photographer, our family had many photographs of relatives and of ourselves, many more than most other families had. I thought about those pictures, now ash beneath our feet. I thought of my mother, who had worked so many days on her knees in our garden, growing sweet tomatoes and juicy cucumbers for our meals. That fertile patch of land was now stripped of life, buried beneath this debris. I imagined my mother safely tucked away in Okayama—I desperately wanted her to be safe—and I wondered if she knew of what had happened. They must know, I thought to myself. I knew she would be wild with fear for me and for my father.

From inside the warehouse, a voice called out.

"Hello there?" A woman stood in the doorway. She waved her arm, beckoning us closer. I thought for a moment that it could be Mrs. Shimazu. It was not. We greeted the woman and her husband. With their two children, they had taken refuge in the warehouse. I think this family must have lived in our neighborhood. They looked familiar to me, but I did not know their names. My father seemed to recognize them. He'd known everyone, and everyone knew him.

The Shimazus themselves were nowhere to be found. I wondered about our other neighbors. The Teshimas? The father was our family doctor, with a practice in the neighborhood. The family lived here in Kamiyanagi-cho as well. I knew their son, who had been one year behind me in school. The Tanakas, the kind family who had offered to shelter us after we'd demolished our house? Their home was gone now, and they were nowhere to be found. Had they survived the blast? And what about Mr. and Mrs. Kake, who provided us the house that became our home for many years? He was old and they were both frail. I wondered if it was possible that they had lived through the explosion.

The family invited us into the warehouse to shelter for the night. I could tell that they were shocked by our wounds. We gratefully accepted.

Upon entering the warehouse, I immediately lay down. I was too exhausted to utter even one word. Finally, I could rest in a safe place without having to get up and move somewhere else. My wounds throbbed, but I also felt intense relief at finally being enclosed behind walls, with a roof overhead, in a place that seemed safer than any we'd been in the past three days. I closed my eyes, and let the conversation of the adults wash over my ears.

I lay listening to my father talk for a long while. He and the couple were sharing stories of what had happened to us all in the blast. I heard my father tell them about fleeing to the river, about the huge fire and the tornado. He told them of the injured masses convening at the drill ground, and of our terrible encounter with the soldiers as we'd attempted to descend from Tosho-gu Shrine.

I marveled at my father's ability to speak of these events as if he had not been a part of them. It felt bizarre to hear him recount our journey almost as if he were a spectator. He sounded like he had already detached himself from the horror. It was strange and disturbing to me. And yet I understood. My father, practical and resourceful, was doing what he had to do to stay alive. In order for us both to stay alive.

I was suddenly struck by a thought that hit me forcefully, and with great surprise: *I am alive.* Wounded, but really and still alive. There had been no time to think about the future in these past three days, so consumed were we with surviving in the present moment, one to the next. But somewhere in the recesses of my mind I hadn't believed that I would make it this far.

I remember stretches of an eerie and frightening silence, a silence that was broken over and over again by screams, cries and howls in the distance outside those factory walls. Howls of pain. Cries of desperation. Screams for the lost.

I remember the popping sounds of explosions that came from fires that still burned across the city. I remember the sound of my father's breathing, heavy and worn. Eventually the adults had quieted, and everyone lay down for the night, my father next to me. Eyes closed, head resting against the floor, my father looked frail to me then. The steely and determined face he had shown me for the past two days had retreated with sleep. His features softened, and became almost childlike. My father, the man who'd kept me moving, who'd kept me alive for the past two days, the man who was determined to get us out of this hell. The man who was brave enough to face those cruel soldiers, and wise enough to stand down from them, so as not to endanger our lives.

I do not remember sleeping, but I must have slept because I recall waking to the most incredible smell. For the first time in three days, my nose registered a scent that was not the acrid scent of burning or death. It was pungent and familiar. It was the smell of miso.

I lifted my head from the floor to see the mother of the family coming toward me cradling a cup of steaming soup. My insides suddenly shook with hunger. I had been so consumed with pain and exhaustion for so many hours, I hadn't thought about food or even felt the impulse to eat. Until now, as I watched this kind woman approach us with miso soup in her hands.

Because of my burns, I couldn't hold a spoon in my right hand. I was too weak to hold the cup. The woman spoon-fed me, gently transferring mouthfuls of warm liquid from a burned tin cup to my waiting mouth. My father, sitting next to me, ate on his own.

Each spoonful of soup soaked into my soul.

My father and I hadn't eaten since that breakfast we shared just moments before the explosion. Three days ago. In that time, the whole world had changed. So many questions arose yet again. What was happening in the rest of the city, in the country? What would today bring? Tomorrow? How would we survive? How would we get word to my mother, to our family, to my brother, and would we see them again? My mind was awash in worry. But for a few moments, as this kind woman fed me soup from a fire-scorched cup, my mind was quieted. My pain was not quiet. My body screamed with it. But in those moments, it felt a little more bearable. Eating that meal restored to me, briefly, a sense of being human.

We were so grateful.

This kind family was not finished helping us. They told us of a shelter that had been established in the Kangyo Bank nearby. They had heard that there were doctors and nurses there, equipped with supplies to treat the wounded. I could tell they were worried about our injuries, especially mine.

The woman had already arranged for help from a soldier to transport us to the bank, where we hoped to receive attention to our wounds. As we ate, we waited with great anticipation for the soldier to arrive. The thought of having a doctor tend to our injuries made me feel hopeful, more hopeful than I had felt in days.

After a short while, we saw a soldier pushing a large carriage bed down the cluttered street in our direction.

We bid our goodbyes to this family that had taken us in and treated us so well.

My father said humbly, "I don't know how we could properly thank you. The miso soup was heavenly. You provided us with shelter. You saved us." We both bowed.

I gingerly climbed onto the floor of the wooden carriage. My father walked alongside. I settled myself as the soldier lifted the carriage handles, pushing me toward the bank building where other injured had gathered. A newfound feeling of hope had arisen within me.

CHAPTER SIX

Teruo

Our hopes of finding medical help were immediately crushed when we arrived at Kangyo Bank.

The bank's thick walls had withstood the blast and were left singed but still standing. The roof was also left intact. The bank's windows had been shattered in the explosion, and the inside floor was covered in pieces and shards of glass. A thick black dust coated every surface and hung in the air. The morning was growing hot. Even with the windows bare and exposed, the room was already sweltering.

What we found was not a temporary hospital, but a dirty room filled with the sick and dying. The place smelled of sweat, burnt flesh, and human waste. Everywhere lay the injured, some wearing blackened clothing, others nearly naked.

There were no doctors. There was no medicine. No food. Only a scant supply of water, far from enough to meet the demands of the crowd that had gathered. No one appeared to be in charge.

My heart sank.

My father said nothing. He simply moved deeper into the room, searching for open space where we could rest.

We found a place for ourselves along one wall and lay down against the hard concrete floor. Hours passed this way. We did not sleep, my father and I. Nor did we speak much. Exhaustion and disappointment came together to render us still and silent.

Every so often I shifted my body this way or that, futile attempts to get comfortable. Even the slightest movement sent pain rushing through my limbs, screaming its way up and down my body. My head throbbed. The length of my right side from my face to my leg felt hot from the inside out.

Beside me, my father was quiet but alert. Thinking, no doubt, about what our next move would be. About how we would survive this day as we had the days before.

All around us, people huddled on the floor. Some were alone, writhing and moaning in pain with no one to comfort them. Others appeared, like my father and me, to have survived with members of their family. Some seemed to have been here for days, in possession of a few tattered and beaten supplies scavenged from the rubble. Others, like my father and me, had nothing.

Many of the people I saw were quiet and did not move at all. I wondered how many were dead already, and how many more would die before this day passed.

Suddenly I heard someone shout my name, "Shinji! Shinji! Is Shinji here? Do you know Shinji? SHINJI! Where are you?"

A teenage boy was running toward me, skipping over people lying and sitting.

It was my best friend Teruo.

His name jumped out of my mouth as soon as I recognized him. How incredible to suddenly see my best friend in this horrible place! Teruo was a colleague of mine in the civilian corps of the army. He was three years younger than I, but we had become great friends. We both worked together at the Department of Headquarters Construction of the Second Army General.

The last time I'd seen Teruo was the day before the bombing. I'd walked to work in the evening to tell my superior that I needed to take

8:15

the next day off to help my family with the demolition of the house. On my way home, I'd stopped off at Teruo's to say hello. It was Teruo who had suggested we go swimming the next night near the Sakae Bridge. It was Teruo who I'd planned to meet on the evening of August 6 for a playful swim in the Kyobashi River. Instead, I wound up standing in the Kyobashi, ducking the winds of a tornado, surrounded by bodies burned like my own.

And now it was Teruo who stood in front of me, alive and healthy.

"How did you find us?" I asked him. It seemed too remarkable, too miraculous to be real.

He'd gone to our house, he said, and encountered the family in the Shimazus' storage building. They told him we'd moved to the bank.

Teruo was adamant that we leave the shelter of the bank. "You can't stay in this place," he said. "There's nothing here." "Where would we go?" my father asked.

Teruo pleaded with us to come to Fuchu. A small village located in the hills east of Hiroshima City, Fuchu was tucked behind a low ridge of mountains that ran from north to south. Teruo's sister had married into a family in Fuchu. He told us that Fuchu had not been burned in the explosion. Teruo himself would be staying there with his sister and her husband's family since, like ours, his family's home in Hiroshima had been destroyed.

He'd heard that the Fuchu Elementary School had been converted into a relief center for survivors. There, Teruo said, we could get medical treatment. He looked worriedly at my wounds.

"We need to get you up and out of here," he said. "You would only be waiting for death here."

He pleaded with us, so desperate to save our lives.

But I couldn't move.

"Teruo, I have no strength left to move an inch more," I said. "Shinji," said Teruo, his face grave. "You cannot stay here. You will die."

I knew he was right. But my body could do nothing.

Teruo, however, would not be defeated. He declared that he would go in search of a vehicle to carry us out of the city, to Fuchu.

"I'll be right back," he called out over his shoulder as he left the bank.

Teruo dashed out of the building like a bullet.

My father and I sat back against the wall of the bank to wait. I didn't know what would happen next. But I knew my friend would not abandon us. Still, I couldn't imagine how he would manage to find us a way out of here amid all the chaos and ruin.

Waiting for Teruo to come back, I thought about our lives before the bombing. I'd finished school at 14 and gone to work. I had been given a job as an apprentice technician with the Imperial Japanese Army. The military trained me to be an electrical technician. I learned about electrical wiring and machinery. I loved to work with machines, to take them apart and put them back together, better than before. Electrical machines were like puzzles to me. I loved to find ways to fix their problems, to solve the puzzle inside of each one.

Unlike my brother Takaji, who was outgoing and full of confidence, I was better with machines. Takaji had been employed by a brokerage before being drafted into the war. He'd be a great businessman someday, I knew. For me, navigating gadgets with wires and switches, no matter how complicated, was easier than making deals and negotiating.

I'd been working at the army armory for five years when, in 1945, the Japanese army set up the Second Army General Headquarters to oversee army operations for the western half of Japan. The military leadership was preparing for the battle against the Allied forces to move to the main islands of Japan. Hiroshima had long been a military city, a strategic location of great importance to the nation. It was then that I'd been transferred to the Department of Headquarters Construction.

Since April, I'd been waiting to be called to army duty. When I was eventually drafted, I would be a technician in the army, repairing and taking care of the military's fleet of airplanes. For a long time, the draft age in Japan had been 20, which was considered the age of adulthood. But the war had put such pressure on the military forces that a year earlier, in 1944, the draft age was lowered to 19, and eventually lowered again, to age 18. As my 19th birthday approached in the winter of 1945, I'd taken my physical exams to prepare for military service. I passed with a good grade, a B+. I was added to the roster, and handed an active duty certificate.

A thought seized me then, lying there on that dirty floor. My certificate! I had been told to have this duty paper secure and available to me at all times. I was to present it upon being drafted. There was real punishment for anyone who lost his certificate. But now mine was gone, burned with everything else we'd lost in the explosion. Even as I lay on the bank building floor, with wounds that prevented me from walking or even standing, I began to worry about how I would explain this error to my superior officers. I wondered what trouble would await me when my superiors found out I'd lost my certificate.

This worry nagged me in my tired and frayed mind, and I couldn't shake it.

At least until I saw a familiar face once again bounding toward us.

Teruo had returned. And he was not alone. He brought a truck and a driver to transport us out of the city to the safety and care of Fuchu. I marveled at how my young friend had accomplished this feat. But that was Teruo: resourceful, energetic, and optimistic, a master in getting things done. My friend was both impulsive and kind, and it made him fearless in asking for help for us that day.

In a tumble of excited words, he explained that he had left us and run directly to the army facility where we had worked together, on the edge of the East Drill Ground. There, Teruo had persuaded a driver into taking a truck out to fetch us.

My father and I were speechless with gratitude.

My friend lifted me from the dirty floor and carried me to the truck outside. My father was able to walk and hoist himself into the vehicle. He settled in beside me. Teruo jumped in as well. He would ride with us to Fuchu and go on to his sister's, where his mother had also taken refuge.

We made the drive slowly out of the city, heading up to the village in the hills above. The distance was fewer than four miles. But the trip took longer than the distance would suggest. So many roads were blocked, rendered unpassable to vehicles. From our place in the back of the truck, we shifted with the vehicle as it lurched and stopped many times before starting to move again. It was evening, and growing dark. The air changed as we moved away from the city. The acrid scent of smoke and burning began to ease. The fine dust and soot that hung densely in the air dissipated.

Eventually we made it out of Hiroshima City, and the roads opened up. The army truck climbed the hills toward the village of Fuchu, toward what I desperately hoped was some small measure of safety and comfort for both my father and me.

When we arrived at the village elementary school, Teruo and the driver helped me from the truck into the building. They guided me toward space in a room that even in the dark I could tell was full of the wounded. My father walked alongside us. I was amazed at his physical endurance. At 63, he was an old man. And yet he'd remained strong for days, despite his age and his injuries.

It was the night of August 9. Four days and three nights had transpired since the explosion. We lay on the hardwood floor inside the Fuchu Elementary School, in a large room that was the school's gymnasium. That night, my father and I held a conversation for the first time, having our first real talk since the morning of the bombing.

"For once we don't have to suffer to move," my father said. I could hear the relief in his voice.

8:15

"How did you know we should go back home?" I asked him. It had seemed a crazy choice, pointless in the thick of all the destruction, and yet returning to the ruins of our home had been just the thing to do. It had been the very act of going home that had led us to where we were now, safe in the hills above the city.

"It must be Buddha who led us in the right direction," my father said. Always looking out for me, he followed this reflection with a warning.

"Don't get too relaxed Shinji," he cautioned me. "You have to keep being strong to endure your pain in the days to come."

I confessed to him that my body felt at its breaking point. The pain was spreading and growing more intense. I was afraid.

"If I could, I would switch my body with yours and take your pain," my father told me. He looked at me with deep concern and I believed he would have done just that, taken my pain as his own, if he were able. It seemed to frustrate him that he could not achieve this impossible feat.

My father shook his head. "Son, the only thing I can do is to tell you that you have to keep your strong will and live on. Don't forget my words."

I promised him I would remember. Now that we were talking, my thoughts tumbled out of me in a rush of feeling.

"Those gatekeeper soldiers," I exclaimed. "They were demons, weren't they?"

I didn't wait for a response from him before continuing.

"I hate them with a passion. They were evil. Maybe even worse than the American bombers. They were our own people, Japanese. How could they treat us that way? I hate those men with a passion," I said, my voice choked with anger.

"Well, Shinji," he replied in his matter of fact tone, "We are in hell right now. No wonder we see demons." Ever practical, my father was

55

calm as he made this frank assessment of the dark underworld and its beings.

That night, my father did acknowledge the cruelty we'd faced. He had faced it even more directly than I, in dealing with those soldiers. But he did not dwell on this evil. Instead, he reminded me of the goodness and kindness that had allowed us to make it this far.

"We saw angels with Buddha's soul last night, too, didn't we?" he reminded me gently. For the cruelty we'd experienced, we'd also been blessed with goodness, in the form of those who'd selflessly helped us to survive.

"Yes, I know, Dad," I replied.

I could not stay quiet. "But I still hate those demons."

I replayed the events of our journey together in my mind. That day at Tosho-gu Shrine, my father had insisted we must go home. So we did. I hadn't believed it would come to any good; it seemed desperate and pointless. But he was right. My father was right about so many things. We'd encountered demons, but we'd been visited by angels as well.

I fell asleep that night with tears of relief in my eyes while imagining the face of the Buddha.

CHAPTER SEVEN

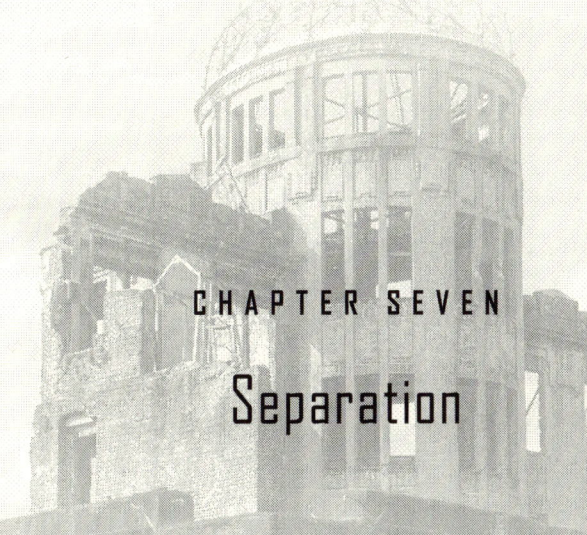

Separation

I WOKE THE NEXT MORNING in agony. The pain of my injuries was growing worse each day. I couldn't have imagined that it was possible to feel such physical suffering and yet remain alive. That morning my father and I had our first chance to see our surroundings in daylight. We were in a large room with at least 50 other survivors. Many were severely injured. There were those who had skin missing from most of their bodies, flesh raw and scorched from burns. Some had cuts and gashes, ugly and gaping, and their limbs looked twisted, broken, and useless. Dozens of faces were covered in burns and were dirty with soot and ash. Those whose faces were not reddened and blackened were pale, eyes sunken, their skin almost blue. Men and women, the very young and the very old. The explosion had trapped them all in its horrible grasp and tossed them aside to suffer.

Like my father and me, they'd made it here, to Fuchu. To what I now fervently hoped was safety at last.

The room was crowded, hot and dense with human odors. We, the injured, lay in rows across the expanse of the floor. There was enough room between rows for people to pass. Here, unlike the Kangyo Bank, there was a sense of order, and of purpose. It seemed as though the entire village was there to help. Girls and women of all ages were moving carefully among the wounded, busy with the work of tending to the sick. Men were hauling sheets and food. Many of the wounded were too weak and too sick to walk, and they were carried outright as I had been the night before. These local men also had the grim task of removing from the gymnasium the bodies of those who had died in the night.

Without any real medical supplies, pieces of household cloth were used for bandages. Wounds were cleaned gently as best they could be.

None of the people tending to the sick were doctors or nurses. But it was clear, even in my pain-ridden haze, that the good people of Fuchu were working with great dedication and sacrifice of their own comforts to help those of us who had been thrust into their care.

What little food that was available was being parceled out to those who could eat. Many were unable to take food. They were simply too badly wounded, too ill to eat or to drink.

That morning, my father and I were visited by Teruo. He was a welcome sight. Teruo was accompanied by his mother. My friend's mother brought food for my father and me: a bit of white rice with *umeboshi*, a pickled sour plum.

This meal was one I'd had countless times before. Hinomaru Bento, the Rising Sun Box Lunch, had been for years heavily promoted by the government during the war years as a healthy meal and a frugal way to eat in difficult and austere times. The dish contains a red pickled plum carefully placed in the center of a mound of white rice and is served in a rectangle box. Its name came from its resemblance to the Japanese flag. Hinomaru Bento was very popular. But as the war progressed, rice grew more and more scarce. It became common to eat Hinomaru with other grains, such as barley or potatoes, white or sweet, in place of rice. Nothing tasted as good as rice though. To have this meal with white rice was a true rarity in these times.

Umeboshi is a food lauded for its potent nutrition. It is thought that this pickled fruit has the power to kill bacteria and fight infection.

Showing great concern for our health, Teruo's mother brought us this very valuable, very nutritious food that she insisted we eat.

My father and I both thanked her profusely.

"This is so kind of you," my father said, a small, tired smile spreading across his face. "Shinji and I are so thankful for this meal."

I took a bite. The *umeboshi* brought a rush of taste, salty and sour, to my mouth. The rice felt both soft and firm under my teeth. This meal, which was so familiar to me, had never tasted like this.

As with the miso soup we'd been given two days before, this food tasted like life itself. It didn't diminish my pain, which seemed to be growing with every moment that passed, but it did soothe me.

We rested that day, side by side, my father and I. The morning was clear and breezy, and occasionally a soft bit of summer wind found its way into the crowded and stuffy gymnasium. It felt like a gentle hand.

My father lay next to me. His eyelids occasionally fluttered toward sleep, but he inevitably snapped his chin forward and raised his head to stay alert. The burns on his face were red and angry looking, and I could tell his arm was giving him pain, the way he held it close to his body. But I could still see determination and focus in his eyes. He looked tired, dirty, and as though he must be hurting badly. But his stubbornness seemed to be winning over his pain and his fatigue. Somehow he continued to fight. Somehow, despite his injuries and his age, he continued to look strong to me.

Later that day, another set of visitors arrived. I looked up to see three men in military uniform striding toward us. My jaw clenched. I was nervous at the sight of soldiers. As the three came closer, I recognized at least one of the men. They were among my superiors at the army armory.

This realization did nothing to soothe my nerves.

We greeted one another, the soldiers, my father and me. News of my whereabouts had reached them thanks to Teruo, who had also communicated to them how badly I was hurt.

"We've come to move you to a real hospital," one of the military men announced.

On Kanawa-jima Island, they told us, a temporary hospital had been set up by the Imperial Army to care for military personnel wounded in the explosion. Kanawa-jima Island was located in Hiroshima Bay, which held the city's port. A decision had been made: I was to be transferred immediately to this facility for treatment.

I was a civilian employee of the army, not a soldier. But I was also what was called *gunzoku*. This means "those who belong to the military." *Gunzoku* was a designation reserved for only certain civilian employees, professional workers who had been trained in special skills, and those skilled workers who were employed full time. Less skilled employees, such as kitchen workers and janitors, were not *gunzoku*. Nor were those who worked part time. We who were *gunzoku* were afforded benefits and a status that did not extend to others. After the bombing, this included access to medical care from the army.

The transfer to a military hospital was good news. The army must have doctors and nurses to treat patients and medical supplies that seemed to be impossible to find elsewhere. But this good news came with difficult news. It was only I who was eligible to be transferred.

My father could not go, the soldiers informed us.

It took a long moment for this news to sink in, for my mind to grasp what they were saying.

My father did not hesitate in his response.

"I will be fine to stay here," my father stated resolutely. He looked me squarely in the eyes.

"You need more help than you can get here, Shinji. I want you to have medical attention right away. You must go."

There was no question that I would go. This was an order coming from my military superiors. There was no choosing whether or not to follow. My pain had only grown stronger and more intense in the days since the bombing. I could feel the pressure of my body filling

8:15

with fluid, swelling taut against the burns that covered my body. I was too weak even to carry my own weight. Walking even a few steps was out of the question. Sitting up to take water or food was almost too difficult to manage. I could barely think. The throbbing in my body took over everything, blocked out my senses, and made me delirious. Continuing as I had been, I would not heal.

What happened next all seemed to happen very quickly. The soldiers had a truck waiting outside to take me to Ujina, a port at the south of the city where I would travel by boat to nearby Kanawa-jima.

My father watched carefully and without expression as my superiors prepared to move me to the truck.

I did not want to leave my father. I was in too much pain to protest or even to think about what was happening at this moment. I could no more imagine being apart from him than I could imagine leaving a part of my own body behind. My father and I had been side by side for days. We had breathed the same smoke-filled air, drank the same dirty water, and stumbled together over the same paths laden with suffering and death. My father's survival and mine were intertwined.

We had made it through these past five days together. But truly, it was he who had carried me through. Perhaps as his son, I gave him a reason to keep going when it would have been so much easier to just be still, to allow life and death to run their course. Perhaps that was my contribution. But it was my father who had navigated every step of our survival.

As the soldiers lifted me from the floor, my father's eyes locked with my own. For just a moment, I thought I saw a shadow of sadness across his face. But it disappeared as quickly as it had arrived, replaced with my father's look of perpetual determination.

"You'll find me at the hospital," I said to him.

He made no response to this.

"Be well, Shinji," he replied to me.

My father's eyes never dropped, never wavered as the soldiers carried me away. Even after I could no longer see him, I could feel him watching me as we parted.

CHAPTER EIGHT

Goddess

I SAID GOODBYE TO MY father on Saturday, August 11. Five days after the bomb. Five days of wandering and navigating our burning, decimated city together. Now our paths had diverged. I was on my own.

The next several days were a painful blur as military personnel moved me from one place to another. My pain continued to worsen. Every day, I thought it could not be possible to feel any worse. And yet the next day, as I woke from whatever fitful sleep I'd managed to achieve, somehow it was – the pain throughout my body had become more intense and unbearable than the day before. Many times throughout these days my sense of time and space slipped away, drowned out by my pain. More than once, I lost track of where I was. For several days, I was nowhere for very long.

The journey began with a difficult start. The soldiers who came for me in Fuchu loaded me into the vehicle for the trip to Ujina port. Stretched out in the back of the military truck as it rumbled along down the mountain roads toward the city once again, I struggled to keep still. It was impossible. Every bump and jolt of the truck sent me pitching and rolling in one direction or another. Even the slightest movement sent ribbons of pain shooting throughout my body.

That day was another in a stifling line of hot and humid days. I squeezed my eyes shut to ward against the sun's glare. I could close my eyes to shield them, but there was no way to shield my body. I could do nothing to keep the sun's hot rays from scorching my raw, burned flesh. I felt as if I were being burned all over again.

I heard the truck sputter and rumble to a stop by the side of the road. Two of the officers jumped from the front of the vehicle, talking animatedly between them. My head was thick with pain and fatigue. I was in little condition to comprehend anything. But it quickly became clear what had derailed our progress. We'd run out of gas. The third officer joined his colleagues on the dusty roadside, and among them they determined a plan. Two would walk on foot back to the Headquarters of the Second Army, at the Onaga Elementary School. The headquarters, on the edge of the East Army Drill Ground, was about a mile and a half away. The third would stay with me at the truck.

The two officers set off in the direction of the Onaga Elementary School. I lay in the back of the truck under the merciless sun. I was so despondent, I might have cried. But my eyes could not make tears. I hadn't the energy to weep. All I could do was take my next breath, and another, as my body roared with pain. There was no part of me that did not hurt.

The sun was relentless. Its heat was merciless on my skin, singeing me where I was already chewed up by burns. My lips were cracked and swollen and oozing with pus. The air I sucked into my throat and lungs felt as hot as a furnace. I felt as though I were cooking right there in the back of that army truck.

The heat also seemed to be getting to the soldier who remained by my side, for it wasn't long before he unbuckled the leather pouch around his waist and removed his jacket, leaving him in his shirtsleeves.

I could barely see as my eyes were forced nearly shut by the swelling that covered my face. My right eye was almost closed, and I could only see blurry shapes and crude movements from my left eye, which I managed to open just slightly. I felt the soldier more than I saw him when he climbed into the back of the truck where I lay immobilized. The next thing I felt was a cooling shade flutter over my swollen face and scorched chest. The officer had draped his jacket over my body to shield me from the sun. This thin veil of fabric brought me profound relief.

I was too weak and consumed with pain to even acknowledge this kind act. I could not speak my thanks, for my mouth was too swollen. I could not lift my hand in acknowledgement of this act of kindness. But my superior officer's kindness did register with me nonetheless, and I felt a surge of gratitude bubble up amid my intense pain.

This kind and selfless act was far from the first I'd been privy to in the days since the bomb. And yet it surprised me. It also made me think again of the soldiers at the Tosho-gu Shrine. Their cruelty haunted me. Their anger and viciousness toward my father and me was mystifying. In this new and damaged world, each act of kindness felt like a miraculous gift. And yet the cruelty and callousness we'd seen and experienced cut deeply. It gnawed down to the bone.

It seemed that the chaos of our circumstances and the collapse of our world had changed our rules. It felt as if the explosion had shaken loose the bonds of civility and propriety that held our lives together. The void that was left behind was pushing people in one direction or another. Some were moved to act with great generosity and kindness. Others veered toward an angry insolence and disrespect, towards indifference and disdain for the welfare of others. I no longer knew what to expect from people. This new reality was, in its own way, as frightening as the physical destruction that had been visited upon us. Our city had been taken from us, wiped out in an instant. Had our character also? What would become of us? Which impulse would we run toward and embrace? Would we ourselves become angels or demons?

I don't know how long we waited in the back of the truck before the two officers returned up the road. But the soldier knelt beside me and shaded me from the sun for the entire time we waited. It felt like an eternity before the other soldiers at last came into view, walking briskly in our direction, each carrying a gas can. We were quickly on the road, headed once again toward Ujina Port.

After our delay by the roadside, we arrived quickly at Ujina. But I would not be there for long. That same day, I was transferred from the military station at the port to Kanawa-jima Island, located just offshore. Kanawa-jima Island was one of several islands in the waters of Hiroshima Bay. The military had been making use of several of these islands. The army had placed a supply depot on Kanawa-jima and now was using the island for emergency medical care in the aftermath of the bombing. Nearby on Ninoshima Island, the Japanese military had housed German prisoners of war during the First World War. Ninoshima was now being used as a place to bring the wounded and the sick who were being quarantined.

The port of Ujina sits at the southern tip of Hiroshima. It was a critical center for military operations in the city that was itself an important linchpin in the nation's military. The port was developed in the 1880s to aid the city's commercial development, a port for shipping and fishing. But it wasn't long before the army seized up on the strategically-located port as a location for operations. The day after war broke out with China in 1894, Japanese military scrambled to build a rail line connecting Ujina port to the trains that were already running in and out of Hiroshima, ferrying soldiers and supplies around the country. Construction took all of sixteen days. Ujina had gone on to become an important supply base and command center for the Japanese Imperial Army in its war against China. The port had remained an active military location ever since. Now, in the war against Japan's latest foes, Ujina housed the Army Marine Headquarters, which was a location of great importance for moving supplies to our army forces.

8:15

    I had been working at Ujina Port in the week leading up to the bombing. In my job at the Department of Headquarters Construction, I was one of a group of ten workers who had been sent to Ujina to work on a wooden ship that floated in the waters of Setonaikai, the Inland Sea. Setonaikai is the nearly 300-mile long body of water that fills the space between three of the four largest islands of Japan, which connects so many of its coastal cities to the broader sea. The ship was being modified for use by the army. It was my job, along with my colleagues, to ferry electrical wires to the ship, then across the sandy, shallow bed of the harbor waters.

    Our work that week had made for long days of laboring. We would report to our regular station at the Onaga Elementary School each morning, then board a truck to travel to Ujina to work the ship and wires for the day before heading back to the school at day's end. I had been scheduled to return to Ujina after the weekend, to continue working with my colleagues on modifications to the army vessel. But I'd taken that Monday off to work with my father to fulfill the Building Evacuation Order handed down by the government. That was the Monday my father and I had been finishing the move to the Tanaka's guesthouse. That was the Monday I sat on the roof of our home in Kamiyanagi-cho, and a bomb exploded and our world collapsed around us.

    I frequently thought about how these past days would have transpired, had it not been for the bomb. I longed for that naivete, the ignorance of not knowing what the real consequences of war were. For a fleeting moment, I thought of what might have happened if I had reported to work as usual that Monday, if I had not taken the day off and been at work at 8:15 that Monday morning, instead of at home. Ujina, at the southern end of the city, was a much greater distance, a little over three miles, from where the bomb had been dropped, in comparison to our neighborhood, at three quarters of a mile. What might have been different? The burns that had ripped through so much of my skin likely would not be here. I would not have spent so many days in desperation, at the mercy of my broken body. My father and I would have been on separate journeys from the beginning. And without me to slow him down, perhaps he'd have found safety sooner.

But this was a pointless exercise. Things had happened as they had.

From Ujina, I was transferred almost immediately to a boat to be ferried to Kanawa-jima Island. I spent a difficult, sleepless night. The next morning, August 12th, brought another leg of my journey, which felt as though it would never end. I was moved again, this time from Kanawa-jima to the beach that stretched behind Koyaura Pier, a small fishing port southeast of Ujina.

It was yet another relentlessly hot day. The beach was sweltering under the quickly rising mid-August sun as I lay amongst other injured military and *gunzoku* personnel. I do not know how many of us were there. I could not lift my head to see anything. Flies swarmed my body, their tiny legs landing on my scorched skin and triggering ruthless waves of pain. I could not lift my hand to swat them away. Even the movement of the sea breezes, which brought welcome cool air, was enough to trigger ripples of pain across my body as they swept over me. I lay at the beach for a day and a night, a thousand individual instances of pain.

The next morning, I was moved once again. Soldiers came and took fifteen of us from the beach to the Koyaura Elementary School nearby. It was here, lying on the school's wooden floor, that my wounds were examined and treated for the first time since the young, inexperienced corpsman at the drill ground had poured a cleanser over my ragged skin. Here, under some direction from the military, volunteers were tending to the injured.

This was not a hospital facility, not even a makeshift one. The care that could be provided was basic, even crude. Supplies were scarce. But the hands that moved over my body were calm and competent

8:15

and sure. They cleaned and wrapped the gaping wound in my thigh, which stretched more than the length of a grown man's foot. My leg was full of infection and had to be drained. A doctor cut open the wound, slicing through my burned flesh to drain the pus that had pooled inside my badly infected leg. They used no anesthesia, not even a painkiller. But I could not feel the pain as the scalpel dipped into my skin. It was impossible to differentiate this pain from any other pain surging through my body. The wound spilled open under the doctor's knife, and with it a lava stream of pus poured out. Maggots were there as well, spilling out of my leg, wriggling amid the ooze. I was too weak to raise my upper body enough to peer down my body. I watched though, as a woman standing nearby ready to tend to me saw the eruption of my leg and hid her face in fear. It was only later, when another attendant helped me sit up so I could try to eat, that I saw my leg. The wound was vast and ugly. It looked as though a range of volcanic mountains had erupted over most of my right thigh.

The room was swarming with flies. Again and again they landed on my body, eating at my raw and infected flesh and piercing me with pain. I could not raise my hand to brush them away. My lips were cracked and caked with dried pus and blood. I could barely open my mouth. My right ear felt hot and tight, as if it might burst at any moment, and throbbed constantly. Even the slightest movement of my head was enough to send a violent wave of pain shooting through my body. The skin on my back was completely gone, most of it burned away in an instant, the rest sloughed off in ragged pieces.

This left my raw flesh sore and stinging with pain.

Each of these injuries would have been difficult and painful on their own. Together, they left me in constant agony. But there was one pain that dwarfed all the others. After so many days of lying prone and unable to move, bedsores had spread across my backside. These ulcerous sores brought a hurt that burrowed deep below the skin and seemed to find me at the bone. This was a pain that made the throbbing of my ear or the raw flesh on my back pale in comparison. It was a pain that made me delirious, that made me feel I might lose my mind. And there was no escaping it. I could not move. The weight of my body put pressure on my sores against the hard and unforgiving wooden floor. My body at this point was emaciated. I was little more than skin over bones. I had always been thin, it was my natural state. And years of going hungry amid wartime food shortages had whittled away even more fat and muscle from my five-foot, eight-inch frame. Before the bomb, I weighed just one hundred pounds. Now, I knew I must be even less. I had no padding on my body to cushion against the hard floor, which made the pain from my sores even worse. It was agonizing.

I did not expect anyone would notice my bedsores. I had so many wounds and was one of so many injured. I was alone. I could not speak, and I had no one to speak for me.

But someone did take notice. A woman from the village of Koyaura was one of the volunteers who tended to me and others of the wounded. She was unremarkable in many ways. Dressed simply, a woman in her late thirties or early forties, she looked like someone's mother. Her manner was calm and sure. She did not seem rattled by my wounds. She fed me with a steady hand, spooning soup into my mouth. I had no appetite. But it felt good to be fed so kindly. She watched me as I struggled to eat. Her eyes narrowed, and her forehead creased when I winced in pain.

Gently, she peered more closely at my wounds. When she saw my sores, she gasped.

"You cannot lie here like this," she said, motioning to the hard floor beneath me, the floor that was a constant agitation to my bedsores. She gathered the remnants of the meal and helped me to settle as best I could on the floor. She clucked again in protest at my wounds.

"You cannot stay this way," she repeated before she left. "I have pillows at home. I'll bring them for you."

8:15

I was too weak to properly display my gratitude. I could only look at her and hope she saw the gratitude in my eyes. With her promise, my heart filled with hope. Hope at the prospect of relief from this most horrible pain. Hope, too, at the presence of such goodness and kindness, such generosity, in the midst of all the horror and death that surrounded me. Now, I had simply to wait for my angel's return.

This waiting felt interminable. Almost as soon as she left, I began to wonder when she might be back. Every minute felt stretched to the length of ten minutes, one hundred minutes. The promise of eventual relief for my sores had the effect of making their pain feel worse as I lay there waiting. I could not turn to the left or to the right. I could see almost nothing of what was happening around me. I could only look straight above, to the worn ceiling that hovered over me. I imagined a kind face above me on that ceiling, a friend who could comfort me and relieve some of my loneliness, and who could share the burden of my pain. As I waited for the woman to return, I talked to my new friend.

The day stretched long in front of me. As the morning slowly passed, I began to worry about the woman's return. I began to wonder if I'd dreamed her. I was in and out of consciousness, and I could almost believe that this calm, caring stranger was an apparition I'd created. With each passing hour, my worry grew more frantic. Was she coming back as she'd promised?

Morning became afternoon, and my worry turned to desperation. I imagined the woman had left my bedside and returned to her home, only to forget the kindness she'd planned to do for me. She'd gotten busy and distracted by the demands of her day, and the pillows had slipped her mind. How could she be so cavalier?

Afternoon became evening. And still, I waited. I was desperate in my pain. I was helpless and alone. My thoughts turned angry and dark. I had believed the word of a stranger who said she would help ease my suffering. I felt rage rise inside me. Rage at being wounded and immobilized. Rage at being alone. Rage at being forgotten. In my weakest state, I had been betrayed by a stranger who had taunted me with promises of kindness and relief. I felt hatred for this woman who had played me so cruelly. She was probably at home with her family, eating a meal, listening to the radio, doing all the normal things my family used to do before our lives were shattered into a million pieces. Perhaps she hadn't even given me a second thought. Perhaps she was a person who made promises as light as summer breezes and discarded them as quickly as those warm breezes pass. I put all of my hope into the promise of this woman, a woman I was now nearly convinced I would never see again. How could she abandon me? What person could do this? I asked these questions to my imaginary friend. He had no answers.

And then suddenly she appeared next to me, and in her arms were zabuton, two square sitting pillows. She was full of apologies for her delayed return. A member of her family had tuberculosis, which at the time was commonly known as "chest sickness." Upon arriving at home to retrieve the pillows, the woman discovered that she needed to tend to her sick family member while the doctor was visiting.

"I'm so sorry it took me so long," she said, as she laid the cushions between my back and the floor. With soft and tender hands, she helped me partially lift my back a couple of inches from the unforgiving floor to stuff them beneath my back.

The moment I saw her, my anger turned to shame. How could I have been so hateful in my thoughts? I was so ashamed to have doubted her, to have become so enraged. I had been right to consider her an angel. She was an angel who had returned to rescue me from my worst pain. She was also an angel who rescued me from the depths of my own judgmental anger.

The thin padding beneath my body felt like a balm to my wounds after the unforgiving floor. It was rapturous, the relief. I felt as though I were floating on clouds. This new comfort brought me so much joy, I bragged to my friend above me on the ceiling: *Look at me, I am sleeping on the pillows.* To my angelic Samaritan, I croaked a thank you from my hoarse throat. Even if I'd had full use of my voice, I could not have found the words to express to her my gratitude. I thought again of the choice that had been forced before us in the aftermath of the explosion. In the wake of such horror and devastation, of such ugly and sorrowful death, what would we become? I could not deny that the scales were tipping to the angels.

Corpsmen were placed at Koyaura Elementary School to tend to the wounded and walked in full regulation uniform, swords sheathed at their sides. One morning, I woke to an unusual sight. It was August 16. This morning, I noticed that these corpsmen were without their swords at their waists. I knew that government regulations demanded that soldiers carry their arms this way at all times, so this change puzzled me. At first I wondered if I had simply spotted an individual corpsman who had somehow neglected to wear his sword. But each corpsman I saw looked the same that morning, all without swords. I asked one of them why he wasn't carrying his swords, and he said the war was over. I asked if we won or lost, and he said he wasn't sure. At this point, I didn't care whether we won or lost. All I felt was a sense of relief.

That morning, a strange energy commanded the room where I lay. It began as a low murmur of voices and rose to a rumble as it cascaded throughout the room. Some people were shouting, angry and defiant. Others were weeping and wailing with tears. Some including myself were silent, eyes and mouths agape, and some were too wounded but others simply too shocked even to speak.

Japan had surrendered. Unconditionally.

The corpsmen I'd seen without their swords had been told to disarm. But even they hadn't known why until the delayed news came to them a day later.

Emperor Hirohito had taken to the radio to tell us himself. At noon on August 15, the day before, this news of surrender was delivered by his own tongue for the ears of the entire nation. The *Gyokuon-hoso*, or Jewel-Voice Broadcast, marked the first time the people of Japan had heard the voice of their Living God. But in Hiroshima, hardly anybody had a radio that was working. The news didn't come to us till the following day.

The Emperor's speech was confusing to many, but the message ultimately became clear. We as a nation must protect the future of Japan by "enduring the unendurable and suffering what is insufferable." We must set aside our pride. We must relinquish our faith in victory against external enemies and redirect that faith toward repairing our battered country from within. We must surrender.

The war was over.

CHAPTER NINE

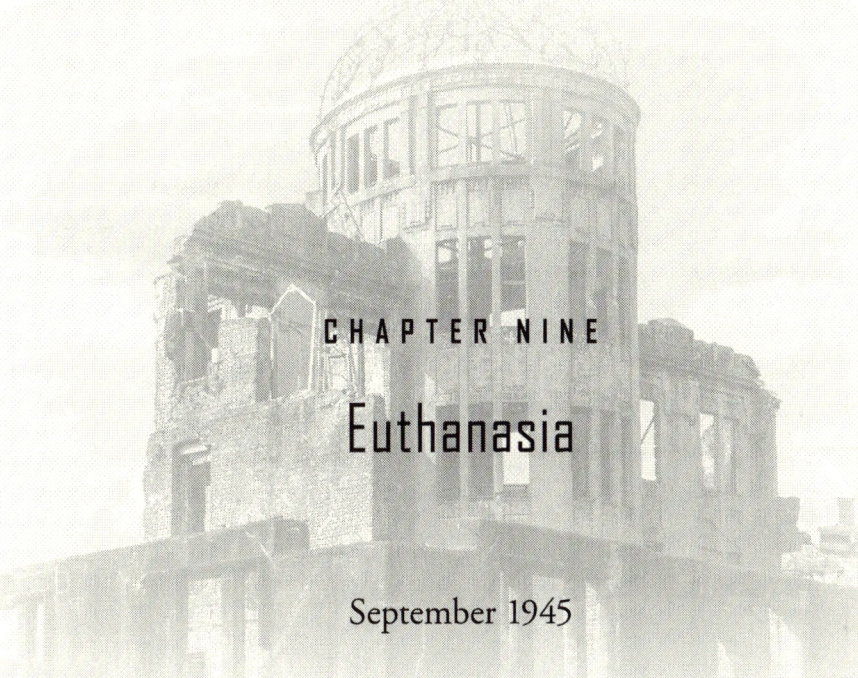

Euthanasia

September 1945

AFTER THE WAR ENDED, I had been transferred to the Ujina Army Hospital. It was here that I stayed and received extended treatment for my injuries. The hospital was overflowing with patients, military and gunzoku civilian personnel. Long rows of beds lined each wall of the ward, and snaked up the middle of the room as well, leaving thin passageways between for medical staff to pass. Every bed appeared to be full. Nurses and aides busied themselves throughout the room. There was no stop to the activity of caring for so many sick and injured. It went on night and day.

Even in this army hospital, supplies were scarce and often altogether absent. It seemed that there was not even sufficient supply of the basic needs: bandages, gauzes, swabs, painkillers and other medicines. There was a constant sense of neediness and not having enough. Nurses and helpers mostly roamed the ward, tending to wounds, soothing the agitated, feeding us, cleaning us and pausing to offer comforting words. The presence of the doctors on the ward was less frequent. There were so few of them and so many of us that they could not linger in any one place. Doctors and nurses had been victim to the bomb just as the rest of us.

A month had passed since the explosion. It was here in the Ujina Army Hospital that I'd learned a second city had been bombed with the same ferocity as our own. Three days after Hiroshima was decimated, another bomb was dropped on Nagasaki, a port city to our south. It had been hit by the same uncomprehendingly lethal explosion. In the hospital, rumors of the nature of this mysterious weapon were flying. Talk abounded of poison gas, of an explosion that did not hit the ground, of a city that would be uninhabitable for generations, and of a lifeless place where nothing would grow for decades. I closed my ears to this talk as best I could. I imagined my father cutting through all this hysterical speculation with his rational, skeptical mind. I tried to do the same, but it was not easy. Fear lodged in me, and I could not make it leave.

I had spent much of the past month staring at the ceiling. My imaginary friend, who first appeared above me in the school in Koyaura, had accompanied me to the military hospital at Ujina. The plain face of the ceiling remained my only companion. It was the most familiar sight to me in those weeks, when moving even slightly was a challenge. As the days and nights went by, I grew to know every detail of my overhead companion. Every divot and crack became familiar to me. No change, however small, to the landscape of my silent friend escaped my attention. A spider web stretching from the corner, a wisp of dust snagged in a rough patch—none went unnoticed by me. I had no choice but to be a devoted watcher. Even after weeks of recovery, I could not walk. I was too weak to move.

In my loneliness and isolation, I gave this blank stretch of ceiling an almost human quality. Looking above, it became a daily habit to silently share my pain and sadness, my worry and fear.

Every morning, I was fed rice gruel from my army-issue bowl, stamped with the military's blue star insignia. I was too weak to feed myself, and my right hand was healing slowly, still useless to me. My appetite was not good and getting worse. But at my nurses' urging, I did my best to work through my bowl.

On many days, as that blue star came into view, I thought of the end of war. I remembered my father's questions about our military leaders' decisions in our prolonged war. I recalled my own uncertainty about the fight to victory that our leaders had promised us. I felt frustrated at our government's denial of the challenges our nation faced in fighting its large and powerful constellation of enemies. I felt disappointed at their refusal to acknowledge we had been losing this war for a long time before it was officially lost. In that time, millions had died, and so many other lives had been destroyed. I was heartbroken because of this great and terrible cost we had paid. These thoughts left me feeling completely lost.

After an unyielding stretch of hot and intensely sunny days that followed the bombing, the weather had turned cloudy and rainy. September was often a rainy month. It was now typhoon season, which could bring rolling thunderclouds and heavy downpours. Dampness had invaded. Everywhere in the hospital ward was a musty smell, even in the thin blanket that covered me. And an ache had settled into my bones.

My broken body was beginning to heal. The swelling in my face and body was receding. The skin across my back, which had been stripped away by the hot burn of the bomb, was beginning to return in tender layers. I could not walk yet, but the wide gash in my leg was starting to close. My pain had started to ease.

But the most intense pain from my wounds had been replaced with another set of ailments. My injuries from the explosion had wounded me from the outside. Now, I was struggling with sickness that was clawing at me from the inside. My hair was falling out in clumps, leaving patches of scalp itchy and exposed. I had a constant fever. I was chilled one moment and dripping with sweat the next.

I had no appetite and could rarely keep food in my stomach when I did manage to eat. Nausea and diarrhea were a constant. Even as my cuts and burns healed, I could feel myself growing weaker. I knew from the nurses who drew my blood that my white blood cell count was skyrocketing. I did not even need to hear the words, after a time. Their faces told me. I was getting sicker by the day.

And I was not the only one. All along the ward where I lay, others were sick in the same way.

In the first days after the bombing, I saw so many people die before my eyes. The day of the explosion, at the Sakae River and the drill ground, I watched as all around me bodies blackened by blast and flame fell to the ground, never to get up. In the downtown bank and the elementary school in the hills of Fuchu, I watched as the wounded grew still. Along the streets of the city, as my father and I traveled back and forth in search of rescue, we saw bodies being thrown together in grotesque piles to be carried away in wooden carriages pushed by corpsmen. They themselves looked tiny and dwarfed by the looming stacks of the dead that they pushed toward one of many cremation sites that had been hastily designated across the city.

As days turned into weeks, the pace of death around me seemed to slow. More of the wounded that surrounded me seemed to be turning away from death toward survival. Like my own, other people's burns slowly began to heal, new skin growing faintly over exposed flesh. Their fractured bones began to set. Their wounds began to stitch themselves together.

But many of the wounded that surrounded me progressed, as I had, only to develop this new illness. The signs were the same. The others around me sweated with fever and grew hollow in the face with nausea and exhaustion. Bald patches spread across their heads, even eyebrows and eyelashes falling from their bodies with the rest of their hair. And they started to bleed from their gums.

8:15

This was a sickness that had come as a result of the explosion. That much was clear. We knew it was a new, different, and more lethal type of bomb, unlike any other that had been used in this war, or in any war. But this sickness did not appear to be connected to the burns and wounds so many of us had received during the explosion itself. It was not always the most obviously injured who became the sickest from this internal disease. It even seemed to puzzle the doctors who treated us. Over and over, patients who did not look as badly damaged from the explosion died while others who had been seriously wounded managed to survive.

This made me think of my father. Not that I needed a reason to think of him. My father was constantly on my mind. I wondered where he was. How he was. When he might find me at the hospital, or how we would otherwise find each other in our demolished city. I tried to take comfort in the memory that we'd been separated once in the chaos of the drill ground and managed to find each other again.

Some of the patients in the hospital had family members who visited them. Mothers and sisters and wives tended to their wounds. They spooned food into mouths and scrounged extra blankets for warmth. I had no one. I was completely alone. I saw patients leave with their families upon their release from the hospital and wondered if I would leave from this place alone. I couldn't imagine where I would go. My cousin Hideko lived in Hiroshima. But I had not seen nor heard from her or her family in the weeks since the bombing. I did not know if they had survived the explosion, or if they were still in the city. I hoped if they were, they had found my father.

I longed for my father's presence by my side. In the days we'd spent together after the explosion, we'd had nothing but each other. In the absence of food and water, a safe place to rest, medicine for our wounds, I'd relied on my father for my very survival. Here, in the hospital, with nurses and doctors to care for me, with enough food to keep me alive, and a roof to keep me safe and dry, I had many things we did not have during those days. But without my father, I felt more uncertain and afraid.

Adding to my fear was a disturbing pattern I'd noticed as more and more people were sickened. At a certain point, for many, the sickness became severe. Fever raged. Gums turned an ugly deep purple, swollen and bleeding. Vomiting wracked the body in spasms. For these patients, nurses seemed to be able to do little to help beyond trying to comfort them. They cooled foreheads with wet cloths, tucked shaking bodies tightly under blankets, and gently coaxed broth into clenched mouths.

And then, inevitably, as the sickness grew to its worst, a nurse would arrive with a syringe. The writhing patient received a shot. It seemed more than a horrible coincidence that all those poor souls who got that shot were dead by the next morning.

I was not the only one who noticed. Among my fellow patients in the ward, this mysterious and seemingly lethal medicine became known as the "euthanasia shot." Patients whispered about it amongst themselves. What was this sinister dose? A mercy killing, decided upon by our caretakers? It was only the very sickest patients who were visited by the nurse with the syringe. It seemed that the nurses who cared for us kindly were harboring a dark secret. This frightening pattern made each of us wary, of them and of each other. So many of us were developing these symptoms. Who would be next?

Patients talked about this mysterious, deadly medication within the ward, but all were careful not to let nurses or other medical staff overhear this anxious speculation. We were too afraid. Not one of us could work up the courage to ask what the purpose of this dark medicine was.

Days passed, my own sickness grew worse. The evening air was mild, yet I shook with chills. My fever was spiking. The last time a nurse had taken my temperature, she frowned and shook her head as she read the stick. It was past 104 degrees Fahrenheit (40 degrees

8:15

Celsius). My white blood cell count had spiked to more than twenty thousand. I could not eat the smallest bite of food or keep liquid in my stomach. My nausea was constant and intense, sending my belly into spasms.

I felt death close by. In the midst of my exhaustion and delirium, I knew I must prepare to meet death well.

After so many endless days of wishing I would die rather than continuing to endure my pain, now I wanted to live. I was afraid to die. I was most afraid to die alone, to never see my family again, and to never know what had become of them all. I thought of my mother and her kindness, my brother and his bravery, and my father and his strength. I desperately wished I could have seen them one more time. Instead, the last thing I would see would be my ceiling friend above me.

But I could not let this fear infect my state of mind. I knew that if the time to hold on to life in this body was over, I must surrender to the current that waited to carry me into another existence. It was the Buddhist way. Death is rebirth. I had spent my life learning the teachings of the Buddha and had tried as best I was able to live a life that was responsible for kindness and respect to others.

Now was the moment I must practice those teachings in the face of my fear. The final moment of consciousness is one of great influence and determination. It is the doorway to the next existence. I struggled to make my mind ready for this letting go, this giving and taking. I created a soft chant in my mind as meditation to replace the fear that could overtake me.

In the dim light of the evening, I saw a nurse come toward me, cradling a needle in her hands. My whole body trembled. Was I shaking from the fever? Or was I trembling in fear? I could not tell the difference. I was almost delirious.

I closed my eyes. "This is it. Goodbye…" I said to myself.

I felt the needle pierce my flesh.

CHAPTER TEN

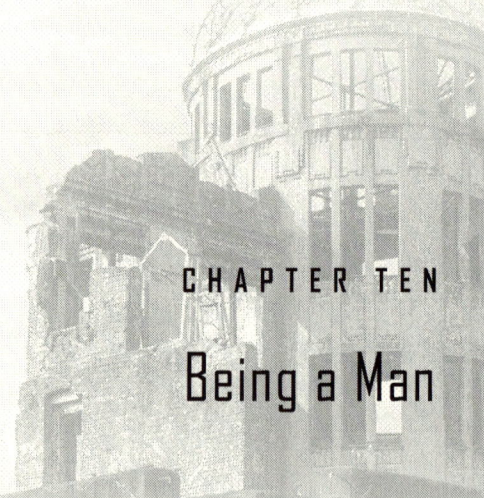

Being a Man

I CRACKED ONE EYE OPEN slowly, feeling disoriented. It took me a moment to get my bearings. I felt the same thin, scratchy blanket covering me. I breathed in the air of my hospital ward: a jumble of scents, potent and ripe, the result of so many bodies sequestered together. My eyes focused on the ceiling above me, that familiar patch of landscape that had occupied my sight for so many weeks. It was then that I knew: I was alive.

The shot I'd feared so greatly had not killed me. Now that I was awake and shifting my limbs about in bed, I realized that in fact I was feeling better. My brow was free of sweat for the first time in many days, and the chills that had made me tremble for hours at a time were gone. My stomach, which had been a roiling sea of nausea, was quiet.

At breakfast, I was able to eat a little. After days with barely any food, the watery porridge in my bowl tasted almost rich. The nurse who took my temperature did not frown as she read the stick like she had for so many days before. This morning was different. She smiled at me.

I was shocked by the change that had overcome me in a single night. The "euthanasia shot" that had inspired such terror had been just the opposite: a life-giving, life-saving elixir. I had energy back in my body. I felt normal again for the first time in a long time. After so many weeks of lying prone and still, to be able to move my body and change my position even to such a modest degree was a miracle to me. It was freedom, an escape from a solitary prison that I'd been held in, trapped by my failing body.

No longer was I locked in a relationship with the ceiling above my head. I bid a hasty goodbye to my "friend."

Some patients were clearly healing, moving from their beds, talking with one another. I could see a great many other patients who were immobilized, as I had been. Many were sick with the internal illness of the explosion. They wretched and sweated; their faces ghostly blue. Others, though, had injuries that rendered them immobilized. Some had scaly and blistered burns that ran from head to toe, sparing no part of their faces or bodies. Others had suffered traumas that had left them damaged and deformed. Bones were exposed under flesh wounds, limbs were ravaged or missing, and faces were obscured by bandages that wrapped grotesque head wounds.

The scope of destruction we'd experienced continued to defy my imagination. It was difficult even to comprehend, despite the weeks that had gone by, despite the ugly and painful evidence now right in front of my eyes. As painful and frightening as my injuries were to me, I could look around this room and feel fortunate to be in the shape I was in.

My body still hurt badly, but the pain had diminished. Pain was a companion that had not left me yet and would not for some time. I was mending slowly on the outside. My frightening internal sickness had finally abated.

The profound relief I felt at my healing was tempered by a loneliness that grew deeper and wider. Now that my mind was no longer completely consumed by my physical pain, my thoughts began to shift. I missed my family. I remembered all the ordinary aspects of our lives together. I thought of the countless meals we'd shared around our table. I remembered sitting around the radio, listening to *rakugo*, a popular form of comic storytelling. My father used to howl in laughter at the voices and intonations of the storyteller as they floated through the radio. The rest of us laughed at our father as much as we did at the program.

Every moment I was awake I wondered what had become of each of them. I imagined my father alone in the city without me. Had he found relatives to help him? Had someone tended to his wounds? My brother could be anywhere. Was he still in the Philippines? When would the army relieve him of his duties and allow him to come home? I was beyond impatient for his return.

I thought of my mother and wondered if she was even still alive. When she left us for Okayama in the summer, my mother was deeply ill with cirrhosis. She was weak and jaundiced. Her belly was swollen with fluid, and she struggled to breathe. The doctor came nearly every week to drain the fluid from her abdomen. By the time my mother left for the mountains, the doctor was emptying her body of nearly two quarts of fluid every visit. I imagined that syringe pricking her swollen skin over and over again.

In truth, she was too sick to travel. But she was afraid to be a burden to us, to my father and me. She could not care for us. She could not care for herself. My mother insisted she stay with her cousin Shigeyo in her home village in the mountains. My Aunty Shigeyo traveled to Hiroshima with her daughter to help my mother make the trip.

Traveling was prohibited, except for the very old and the very young. But my mother's sickness was such that she was given permission and a certificate to leave the city and return to Okayama with her cousin. Unfortunately, the ban on travel meant that my father and I would not be able to visit her.

Each of us knew what this separation would likely mean. My mother's illness was severe. Our goodbye that day might be our last. None of us spoke of this to each other, but I knew I might never see my mother again after that day.

8:15

This was not the first time my family had been fractured and separated from one another. After my birth mother, Chiyono, died, I was sent away from home to live with her uncle. My great-uncle Seishiro took me to live with him. My brother Takaji, at nearly six years old, stayed with my father. But I was not yet three, and too young to stay in my father's care. So Seishiro stepped in.

His kind act was a fulfillment of my mother Chiyono's last wishes. In the last days of her illness, Chiyono called Seishiro to her bedside. When he arrived, she was weak and could barely breathe. She was reluctant to speak, but Seishiro knew that his niece had something to ask him. He pressed her, urging Chiyono to ask for his help in any way she needed. But she refused to impose on him. She would not utter her wishes aloud.

It was no more than a few days later that she died. At Chiyono's funeral, Seishiro heard a neighbor couple say that they would be raising me as their son now that my mother had died.

Seishiro went to my father and questioned him on the matter. "We haven't made any promise," my father told him. "But they have been asking to take Shinji to raise him as their child."

Seishiro knew then what my mother Chiyono had wanted from him as she lay dying, what she had been unable to ask. He turned on his heel and sought out the neighbors. Taking the couple aside, Seishiro explained that he'd made a promise to Chiyono to care for her youngest son, to raise him upon her death. It had not exactly happened this way, but Seishiro was certain it was what his niece wanted.

"I'm sorry," he announced to the couple. "But I am taking Shinji home."

And so I left my father and my brother. I went to Kure City with my great uncle to live with him and his wife. Seishiro was well off, and his home was a comfortable one. He and his wife were kind to me, I know. But I was too young to remember life with my great uncle.

Seishiro was a reliable man and a kind one. He was not done using his influence to protect my young life. During the months after Chiyono died, Seishiro began prodding her sister, Nami, to marry my father. Nami had been married and divorced from a man who was dishonorable. When her sister Chiyono died and I went to live with Seishiro, Nami was living on her own in Kyoto making a living sewing and selling kimono.

Seishiro urged her to consider the marriage to my father. You're not getting any younger, he reminded her. She could care for Takaji and me, he suggested, and be assured that she would not be alone in her old age without anyone to care for her. This sort of marriage was exactly the kind of practical arrangement that was commonplace among families.

Yet, Nami resisted. She did not believe that she would get along with my father, but Seishiro would not give up. It did not happen quickly, but over time and with Seishiro's persuasion, Nami agreed to marry my father, Fukuichi. In the end, it was her sense of caring and duty for me and my brother that made Nami relent. She understood that as long as my father was unmarried, I could not live with him and my brother. With a woman in the house willing to care for the children, I could go home. Just before I entered elementary school, she married my father. And I returned home.

I was so young when all this took place that I came to know of these events, so consequential to my life, mostly through stories and not my own memory. I remember only bits and pieces of the time before my family was my father, Nami, and my brother. When I began truly to know myself in the world, it was with these three people in a house in Kamiyanagi-cho.

Takaji and I had always called Nami "Aunty." Now, with her marriage to my father, she had become our mother. But we continued to call her aunt. It was what we were used to. For all the years we lived together as a family, Nami was "Aunty." Even after we grew to think of her as our mother, we still used "Aunty." When the war came, and we knew we would be drafted, my brother and I made a pact. Should we come home alive from fighting, and be able to return to our family, we would begin to call Nami what she was. Mother.

Had I missed my chance?

It was questions such as this one that consumed me as I lay in the hospital. Now that I was feeling better, my mind was sharper. I could not stop it from turning. My thoughts were like a blade cutting into me over and over again.

Most of my burns and other wounds were healing, but my right ear was not. Instead, the pain there grew worse. This ear, which had given me pain and trouble since the moment the explosion threw me from the roof, had swollen into a massive orb. Misshapen from the swelling and scarlet red, it ached and throbbed constantly. The doctor who examined me told me that the cartilage inside my ear had become infected. The infection was advanced and could not be remedied with medicine. There was only one way to stop the infection and curtail the pain. He must remove a large section, about one-third of my ear.

The prospect of surgery frightened me. But I was more afraid of prolonging this pain, which had once again sent me into unimaginable depths. I'd had a brief taste of relief from the worst of my pain, as my symptoms had subsided and my wounds begun to heal. Now, this infection had thrown me back into a state of pain that roared constantly. I was desperate for it to cease.

I tried to summon my bravery in preparation for the operation. I was not like my brother, who was naturally brave. As a child I was sickly. Takaji was strong. I was shy. My brother was bold. Takaji had many more of the characteristics of my father than I did. They were alike in many ways. Bravery, I knew, was one of their shared genetic traits.

I missed my brother's leadership, even if it had often turned to bullying. My brother had bullied me when we were children, but his bossiness with me was infused with kindness and his sense of humor. Once I was old enough to understand it, I admired my brother even for the ways he ruled over me.

Once when we were still small children, my brother broke a cherished toy of mine. I could not have been more than six, and Takaji eight. I had a wooden plane that I loved more than any other toy in our house. Unbeknownst to me, Takaji snuck this toy of mine away to play with on his own and broke it. He must have known I would be devastated. He was too proud to confess directly. But he also could not bring himself to pretend to know nothing of the toy and its demise. So he crafted a scheme that would make him confessor and hero at the same time.

Takaji gathered up the broken pieces of the wooden plane and stuffed them under the cover of a futon. Then he went in search of me.

"Hey Shinji," he called out. "Come look at this." He told me of a strange shape growing out of the futon. "It's really spooky," Takaji said. "It might be a monster."

I was a timid child, easily frightened. The thought of a monster in the futon seemed both plausible and terrifying. I begged my brother to use all his strength and bravery to investigate this strange and threatening presence.

Takaji played along. "If you beg, fine," he replied. "I'll be a good big brother and discover what this mysterious thing is for you."

He crept toward the bulge as if it were a serpent ready to strike, sneaking careful steps in one at a time. I hid behind my brother's back, quaking with fear and fascinated by both the mysterious hidden creature and my brother's great bravery.

With a grand gesture, Takaji pulled back the futon cover to reveal the wooden plane in pieces. My response was just as he'd anticipated. I was so relieved that the monster was not real that I did not stop to wonder about how my beloved plane had broken. All I felt was gratitude to my brother for protecting me and unmasking the mysterious threat.

8:15

It took me a long time to realize how he'd rigged the situation to his advantage.

How I wished Takaji could protect me now from all the things that frightened me. I did not feel heroic here alone.

I was moved to a different ward for surgery, and set up next to another patient, a woman who also needed an operation. As a nurse swabbed at my tender ear in preparation for the procedure, the doctor who would perform the surgery arrived, carrying a syringe full of anesthetic. The doctor and nurse talked over me as they worked. I lay there, trying to be still and calm. I heard the doctor tell the nurse that the dose of anesthetic in his hands was the very last available in the hospital. None of the patients who were waiting for procedures would have the benefit of anesthesia.

My initial feeling was one of relief. How lucky I was. I glanced over at the woman next to me. She was in terrible condition, and in excruciating pain. Nearly naked, her body was covered in sores and wounds that were badly infected. Hundreds of razor-sharp shards of glass remained stuck in her flesh. She, too, was awaiting surgery. My feeling at my good fortune shifted. I could not feel relief in taking the anesthetic, knowing it meant shifting pain to another.

I looked at the doctor, who was about to give me the shot. "Wait," I said. "Do not use this for me. Please, give it to her."

I gestured to the woman next to me. "I am a man. She is a woman with more wounds. I must keep my honor and bear the pain."

The doctor and nurse stared at me for a moment. He asked me, "Are you sure?" He warned me of the pain, and reminded me that he would be cutting away a substantial portion of my ear.

I told him to proceed without the drug. The first cut rocked me. I felt the blade tearing through flesh, making my head ring out in agony. The doctor worked as quickly as he could, but his deftness with a scalpel could not help me escape the pain. I convulsed with it. I screamed through a clenched jaw. I longed to lose consciousness as the cutting went on, pulling away infected cartilage. But I was not spared a moment of awareness as the doctor excised the diseased flesh from my body.

Only when it was over, my head bandaged, did I drift into a dreamless stupor, exhausted by the pain my body had just endured.

CHAPTER ELEVEN

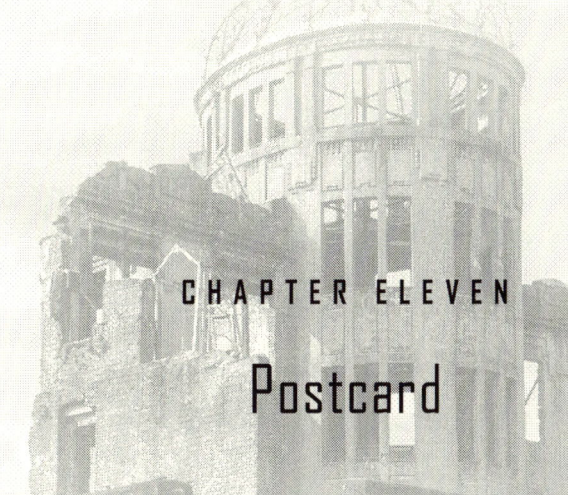

Postcard

The right side of my head seared with pain. The doctor had successfully removed the infected portion of my ear. What was left was a ragged, misshapen mess. Surgery without anesthetics had left me weak and exhausted.

The pain made sleep difficult, nearly impossible to achieve. I lay in bed counting the minutes until I might sleep again, to be away from the incessant, aching pain even for a short while.

In the bed next to me was a soldier about my age. He was from Tokyo, but had the misfortune to be in Hiroshima on the day of the explosion. His mother had traveled from Tokyo to tend to him. She was a constant presence at her son's bedside. She watched his wounds and changed his bandages, which she carefully washed and dried so that she could use them again and again. She made sure his food was available to him, feeding him warm soup. She cleaned him, sponging carefully around his burns. She sat by his side as he slept, watchful and alert, her attention given away only to the needlework she kept in her lap.

I still had not seen or heard from anyone in my family. Now that the surrender had taken place, my brother surely would soon be coming home. I knew it might take time for his squadron to make its way back from the Philippines. But I was impatient for him to arrive.

For as long as I was stuck in the hospital, I could do nothing to seek out our father. If Takaji were home, he could take up the search.

Teruo had visited me, bouncing into the ward unexpectedly one morning, full of energy and news of the city. Hiroshima, decimated as it had been, was scratching out a return to life in fits and starts. Trains were running. The local and prefectural government had reorganized and was operating out of temporary quarters, including a partially damaged temple, on the outskirts of the city. Their headquarters in the city center had been destroyed in the blast. People began returning to the city in the first few days after the explosion to survey the damage to their homes, continue looking for missing loved ones, and to try to pick up the shattered pieces of their lives. Others were there to scavenge in the rubble. They built ramshackle barracks to live in. Policing of the city was slowly improving as the local and national government mobilized in an attempt to restore some basic order. Chaos continued to reign, however.

Rumors abounded about the nature of the bomb that had been dropped on us, just as they did in the hospital. The newspapers had published reports that the weapon was an atomic bomb, a new and lethal weapon that carried the force of two thousand B-29 bombs. It was said that no plant would grow in the city for seventy years because of the lasting effects of radiation.

The Americans were expected at any time. We were to be an occupied nation, subject to the terms of the treaty signed by Emperor Hirohito in the wake of surrender. Our military was to be dismantled, and our government was to be re-organized, all under the direction of the U.S. and Allied command. It was a dizzying picture to contemplate from inside the confines of the hospital walls.

Other than Teruo, I had seen no one else in the weeks I'd been in the hospital. I had only a handful of relatives in the city. I continued to wonder what had become of them. My cousin, Hideko, lived with her husband and family in the Ozucho section of Hiroshima. Their

8:15

neighborhood was located some distance from the worst destruction of the bomb. I was hopeful that they had survived without injury. Ozucho was not far from Fuchu, where I'd last been with my father before we were forced to separate. I had so many questions for my cousin. Had Hideko and her husband been able to find my father? Had they taken him in, found him medical help? Who would find me?

My father and mother had been exceptionally kind to Hideko and her husband, extending to them many favors to help them establish their lives. This was typical for my parents. Both my father and mother were instinctively generous people. They took their responsibility to care and watch over their families very seriously. My father was a fixer, a man who was helpful by nature. Growing up, I'd watched him open doors of opportunity for many young people.

My mother was a deeply caring and giving woman. When she married Fukuichi, my father, she took on the responsibility of caring for Takaji and me. She had committed to that duty without reservation. Nami loved and cared for us as a mother would. And we weren't the only ones who benefited from my mother's kind and nurturing nature. When it came to family, and especially children, my mother's generosity knew few limits.

Nami and Chiyono's youngest brother was Torao. Growing up, Torao was a hero to me. I looked up to him and admired him greatly. Torao had attended the very selective Naval Engineering School in Kure City, the only school of its kind in the whole country. He graduated as valedictorian of his class. I remember him visiting us often when he was living in Kure City. He always brought Takaji and me wonderful toys and played with us. Once he presented us each with our own baseball glove, a very rare and special gift in those days. It became a prized possession. I remember Torao visiting after his graduation and showing me the gold watch he'd been given in recognition of his first-in-class status. A child could not have looked up to an uncle more than I did Torao.

After graduation, Torao joined the Ministry of the Navy, where he was steadily promoted. He was transferred to work in Tokyo, which meant, to my disappointment, that we saw him less frequently. Eventually, Torao married a woman from a prosperous family. Our entire family was proud of Torao's success.

When Torao's wife became pregnant, he asked Nami to come and help prepare for the birth. I remember that my mother left for Tokyo shortly before the end of the calendar year. That year, our New Year's celebrations were in disorganized shambles without my mother to cook and orchestrate the holiday festivities. She returned home to us in March. With her, she carried a great surprise.

Torao's wife had given birth to twin girls. The new mother was overwhelmed at the prospect of caring for two babies on her own. Nami offered to care for one of the infants herself. She carried the baby sleeping on her back on the train ride from Tokyo to Hiroshima.

Kiyoko lived with us for three years. Takaji and I loved having her with us. She was a little sister we doted upon. And Nami poured her heart into caring for Kiyoko just as she cared for us. None of us were her children, but no one could ever have known. Neighbors who assumed that Kiyoko must be Nami's granddaughter were shocked when they found that the child was her niece.

"It's hard enough to raise our own children and grandchildren," the women exclaimed. "How could you possibly devote yourself to your niece?" Little did they know, the boys they thought were Nami's own sons were not sons but nephews.

Eventually, when it was time for Kiyoko to return to her parents in Tokyo, Takaji and I were bereft. We begged our parents not to send her away. My father insisted it was the right thing to do, that she was old enough for her mother to care for her along with her twin sister. When we continued to protest, my father grew firm.

"Kiyoko is not a puppy," he scolded us. "Unless you can be fully responsible to raise her until we can send her to her future husband and his family, we can't keep her just because she is adorable. Your mother and I are old. It would be an irresponsible thing to do." My father's sense of justice and fairness ran as deep as my mother's nurturing kindness.

In the hospital, I watched as the mother of the soldier next to me put all of her energy into caring for her son. I knew that if she could, my mother would be here for me doing exactly the same. I could see that the soldier's mother pitied me. I found her stealing glances in my direction throughout the day. She gazed at me with a worried face, as she watched me lay still and silent. I could see my solitary existence reflected in her sad eyes. She slept by her son's bedside each night. Each morning when I woke up, she greeted me with a smile and often asked me how I was feeling. But the sadness never left her eyes.

My solitude made me restless and anxious. I was not yet well enough to think of leaving the hospital. I could not even walk yet. But I was desperate for news of my father and mother, and of my brother. I wished I could will my legs to work, so I might jump from my bed and race back to Fuchu to retrace my father's steps in the weeks since we parted. So that I might return to the army headquarters in search of information about where my brother was now that the fighting had ceased, and when he would be coming home. So that I might make my way out of this charred city to Okayama, on the slim chance that my mother was still alive.

One day, the soldier's mother broke from her maternal vigil and turned to me with an excited smile. She had performed her typical ritual for the morning, preparing and feeding her son breakfast, turning the pillows underneath him, washing bandages and hanging them to dry. After a time, her son was resting comfortably and there was a lull in her work.

She pulled a postcard from her things and waved it in front of me. She'd been thinking about my situation and had the idea that she could help me send a postcard to my family. Mail was operating again, but there were no supplies like this available in Hiroshima. The woman had brought postcards with her from Tokyo so she could stay in touch with her family. With her postcard, I could write to anyone I wanted.

"Who would you like to write?" she asked me.

I knew I must write to my mother. If there was any chance she was still alive, I needed to reach her and let her know I was safe. I was happy and grateful for her offer. But just as quickly, I realized my own limitation. I looked down in shame.

"What's wrong?" the woman asked me. "I've already written to my family, so it's okay for you to use this last postcard."

"Thank you so much for your generosity," I mumbled. "But I can't use my right hand yet, so I cannot write."

The woman brushed my worries away like shooing a housefly. "Oh, I'm sorry. I didn't think of that. I should have offered to write for you. It's no problem."

I had no words to express my gratitude for her kindness.

The woman's steady hand scrawled across the card as I dictated my simple message.

September 2, 1945

Dear Mother,
I have sustained bad burns on my face, right arm, back and right thigh, but I'm OK now. I should be able to come visit you around the end of September. Please be well and wait for me.

Dear Aunt Shigeyo,
I'm so glad we didn't get bombed when you came to pick my mother up at the end of July. Thank you so much for making such efforts and taking good care of my mother. My neighbor is taking dictation for me.

Shinji Mikamo

8:15

She agreed to mail the card immediately. I wondered how long it would take to reach my mother's village in the mountains, and if it had any hope of getting there in time.

CHAPTER TWELVE

Discharge

I HAD SENT THE POSTCARD to my mother out into the world. I could only hope that it might find her, alive, in Okayama. It seemed impossible. She had been so sick when I had last seen her, and that was now many weeks ago. The chances seemed grim and small. But I could do nothing but hope. I also hoped that reaching my mother— and her caring family in the mountains—might somehow bring me closer to reuniting with my father and my brother. I wondered if my father had managed to get word there himself. As the weeks went by, I felt ever more desperately cut off from the world.

Soon, it would be time for me to leave the hospital. My recovery was plodding and often frustrating, and much slower than I'd have liked. But I was healing. My right side, which had taken the brunt of the heat from the blast, had been stubborn in its recovery. My arm was stiff with pain. I could barely bend my elbow. I could not so much as hold chopsticks in my right hand. The side of my head still ached from the infection and operation on my ear. And I was just beginning to get my legs back underneath me. It had taken me many weeks, but I was starting to walk. Most mornings, I took a few, hesitant steps along the crowded hospital ward, trying to rebuild my strength. My legs were weak and atrophied from so much time in bed. My muscles felt wobbly and unreliable. The gash on my right leg had closed, but the wound had left my thigh muscles sore and compromised. I hadn't regained much of my speed or strength, but my body was repairing itself.

I spent most of my days and nights in silence, and in a state of restless worry. My emotions were divided. I was anxious to be well, well enough to leave my hospital bed. At the same time, I was frightened by what awaited me at the end of my hospital stay. My family home had been destroyed. With the war ended, I no longer had a job at the army armory. My injuries were still serious enough that they were likely to interfere with even the simplest labor. I could not lift any weight with my arms. My right hand was weak and without a grip. I could not hold the tools of my electrical trade. My fingers were still and slow, without the dexterity that I'd once taken for granted. I'd never thought before about the nimbleness that had once allowed me to navigate a complicated tangle of tiny wires on an electrical board. My nimbleness was gone, and I did not know when, or if, it would return.

I was consumed with worry for my family. This was not new. I'd done little else but think of them. Increasingly, as my body healed and my release from the hospital drew closer, I also worried about how I would manage on my own. Each day that brought improvement to my health also delivered to me new fear and uncertainty. I was lucky to be alive. I knew this. And yet I felt frightened and deeply adrift. I had no idea where I would go, or what I would do to survive. I did not know where to begin. I needed my brother badly. I was worried that I'd still heard no news of him. Teruo had said that soldiers were beginning to return from the front, but many others were still waiting to be released from service. My friend had not seen nor heard word of my brother, but he'd promised to remain alert for any news.

The doctor who treated me in the hospital was kind. He knew what circumstances awaited me when I was well enough to leave his care. He knew that I was alone, that I had nowhere to go, and no one looking out for me. When it became clear that I would not need to stay in the hospital much longer, my doctor told me I could extend my stay by a little while, if I needed to. This was a relief to me, and I was grateful for his generous offer. But I also knew that extending my stay for a few days, or a week, was not the answer to my problem. I had hoped that my brother would be home by the time I left the hospital. As the day drew nearer, I watched for his arrival with growing anxiety.

One day in the middle of October, I saw a familiar face walking toward me down the ward. It was my cousin, Hideko. The sight of my cousin filled me with great cheer and hope. Someone from my family had come for me at last.

Hideko arrived with her 12-year-old daughter Machiko. The girl trailed behind her mother as Hideko arrived at my bedside. We greeted each other warmly, but I could see wariness and concern in my cousin's face.

It disappointed me to see her frown. As we talked, I began to understand what lay behind her worried look.

It was only natural to think that I would go to stay with Hideko and her family upon my discharge from the hospital. They were my only relatives in the city. For all the weeks I'd lain in the hospital, I had hoped this would come to pass. Now, with Hideko's visit, I could rest assured that this would be the case. Hideko also expected that I would stay with her family in Ozucho after I left the hospital. This was simple, a family duty.

But for Hideko, it was not so simple. My cousin was married to a very difficult man. He was odd, always shunning the company of others and preferring to be alone. He was insecure, and did not want his wife's attention diverted from him. And he was mean, lashing out at anyone who intruded on his strange routines. I suspected that Hideko was anticipating the difficulty my presence in their home would pose to her husband.

"Shinji, you must make sure you are recovered as much as you can be before you come to us," Hideko warned me. "We don't have a doctor nearby."

I understood her warning. My stay in her home would be better if it were shorter, and if I required as little attention as possible while I was there. Hideko did not want me to leave the hospital before I could take care of myself, which included looking for a job and my own place to live, without delay.

I wondered if Hideko had seen or heard word from my father, and I was eager to ask her about what she knew of him. It surprised me that she had made no mention of him since she'd arrived. As it turned out, I did not need to ask. My question was answered for me, and not in the way I had hoped.

Machiko, who had been standing quietly at her mother's hip, had been looking at me quizzically throughout our visit. She turned to Hideko and asked: "Where is Grandpa?"

Hideko looked suddenly stricken, her face contorted with shame. She quickly hushed her daughter. My cousin could not meet my eyes, her embarrassment was so strong.

My heart felt as if it had been dropped to the floor. Dismay rose in my blood. For in that moment, I recognized what the girl's innocent question had revealed. Hideko and her family did not know where my father was. They were the only family in the city who could have sought him out and helped him after I left him behind in Fuchu. If Hideko didn't know where my father was, nobody did. And left alone for all these weeks, wounded in the depraved conditions of the city, my father had most certainly perished.

I was shocked. Hideko and her family lived in Ozucho, which was removed from the most serious damage of the bomb. Their neighborhood was not far from Fuchu. Traveling to the Fuchu Elementary School, where my father had been, was as simple as a half-hour walk, or a ten-minute bicycle ride. Yet somehow, Hideko and her family had not managed to find my father, or to provide him with shelter, or help of any kind.

My mind was lit with questions. Had they looked for him but not been able to find him? Had they not even bothered to try? I couldn't imagine that such dereliction could be true. My father and mother had been so generous to Hideko and her family over the years. Gratitude, in addition to duty, had to have prompted them to make some kind of effort to seek out my father and offer him help. And yet, they had not made contact.

Hideko shuttled her daughter away from my bedside. She was still avoiding my eye as she left the hospital ward. I was left to wonder, with less hope than I'd felt in weeks, about how my father had managed alone, and what had become of him.

As the day of my release from the hospital approached, I grew even more anxious. The prospect of living with Hideko and her strange, standoffish husband made me nervous. I had clung for so many weeks to the hope that my father had found a way to survive on his own. I knew that Hideko and her family were likely his best chance of rescue. If they hadn't found him, how could he survive, wounded as he was, among so many strangers? Who would notice one wounded old man among so many thousands?

* * * * * * *

The day before I was to be released from the hospital, I had a visit from an old friend. I had known Kunio since we were in elementary school together. We had stayed in contact after we graduated from school and both went off to work.

Kunio's family operated a *dagashi-ya*, a candy store, in Hiroshima. I had visited their storefront many times as a child. I could still recall my thrill at the sight of colorful sacks and jars of sweets and confections, all lined up one after the next. At the time it seemed to me the most wonderful job in the world, to work in such a store. As the war dragged on, sugar became scarce, then altogether impossible to acquire. Kunio's family was in the unenviable position of operating a candy store with no candy. They managed to scrape by, selling whatever they could get their hands on, including toys and other assorted trinkets.

My spirits were buoyed by Kunio's visit. It was good to see a friend. I felt slightly less alone in the world. Kunio asked how he could help. He knew that I was to be released the next day. I did not want to bother my friend, but I had to ask him if he could bring me some old clothes. I had nothing to wear when I was to leave the hospital. He gladly agreed. He also promised to meet me at the hospital the next day and accompany me to Hideko's house.

That night, I barely slept. As lonely as I'd been, the hospital had also become a place of security and safety. The unknown awaited me on the other side of its doors. With my body still frail, I hardly felt equipped to meet them. More than anything, I wished my brother were there. I must be strong on my own until he arrived back in the city.

That morning, a man from my army unit at the Second General Headquarters came to see me. He brought me a change of clothes. The clothes were simple civilian dress. I could tell they were old and had been heavily used, the fabric thin and worn in patches. The officer then handed me a wad of money, about 500 yen. This was more than a whole month of pay at my old job at the army. Being *gunzoku*, a civilian employee of the army, had entitled me to these benefits. A nurse at the hospital also provided me with a blanket. I don't know whether they did this for everyone. I think not. My caregivers all knew I was leaving the hospital without a job or prospects, without family connections, without a home to return to. A set of clothes, a blanket, and a month's pay in my pocket. These were the possessions with which I would re-enter the world.

As promised, Kunio arrived back at the hospital to help me get to my cousin's home in Ozucho. He brought me another set of clothes, not nearly as worn as the ones the army had issued to me. I gladly changed into the clothing that Kunio gave to me, and stowed the other set with my hospital blanket. In a moment, I'd doubled my entire wardrobe.

Together, Kunio and I walked to Hideko's home in Ozucho. After so many weeks indoors, it was a novelty to feel the sun's warmth and the crisp breeze from the harbor. I moved slowly, and my gait was still weak and unsteady. My right arm was still stiff and difficult to bend. If I stumbled, I would not be able to break my fall. Kunio stayed close to me as we walked slowly away from the hospital.

I had not seen the city with my own eyes since just a few days after the bombing. In more than two months, much had changed. The air was clear now of the acrid stench of fire and burning flesh which had been everywhere in the first days after the explosion. Amid the towering rubble that remained, activity had returned to the city streets.

The Americans had also arrived. Thousands of U.S. soldiers had flooded the country at the beginning of October to oversee that the terms of the surrender were carried out, and that our country's military was dismantled. We were now an occupied nation. There were no U.S. soldiers staying in Hiroshima. The city was too destroyed, there was nowhere for them to stay in the city itself. But from Kure City and other nearby stations, American soldiers traveled to the city. It was not a surprise that the U.S. military would be here in our city. This reality was an inevitable part of our defeat, but it was still unsettling to see foreign soldiers on our streets.

Kunio and I walked through neighborhoods where the bomb had wrought lesser damage. Even in these places, a coating of ash held stubbornly to many surfaces. In some places, it was as thick as snow drifts. As we walked, our route grazed sections of the city that had seen more serious devastation. In these areas, whole streets' worth of buildings had crumbled under the pressure and heat of the explosion. Even in these neighborhoods, signs of life were plentiful

8:15

amid the destruction. Makeshift dwellings had cropped up. Resilient survivors with nowhere else to go had strung together salvaged sheets of metal, wooden boards, and unbroken roof tiles to create shelters. Families cooked meals on fires in the open. There were no storefronts left in these places to sell goods. In their place had arrived a different sort of commerce: sellers were peddling whatever provisions they had collected from open carts. Schools had reopened throughout the city. Without buildings to house their lessons, classrooms were held in the open air.

Kunio and I said our goodbyes at Hideko's front door. I thanked him for his help. I felt lucky to have him as a friend.

My stay at Hideko's was short, shorter even than either of us might have imagined. Her husband was cruel and dismissive to me. In what I gather was her attempt to keep the peace in her home, Hideko largely ignored me as well. I tried to make myself invisible, to leave the lightest footprint possible in my wake. But I knew from their demeanor that I was not welcome.

I turned to Kunio and other friends for help. They let me stay with them for many of those nights after my discharge. Hideko's house was full of tension and discord, and my presence was the cause. I was not surprised at all when, only ten days into my stay, Hideko approached me with news.

"I have negotiated a room for you in our neighbor's house," she explained. It was a room the size of six tatami mats, about nine by twelve feet. She encouraged me to move there immediately. I understood that this was not a request, that I had no choice. I did not feel angry toward my cousin. I could see clearly the difficult life that she led, and the misery that her husband brought to their lives. But I did not understand how she and her husband could behave with such selfishness, especially in the wake of the kindness my father and mother had extended to them.

I had nothing to pack. I gathered my few belongings, including my money carefully stowed. I moved to my new living quarters, my heart heavy with the knowledge that my only family connection in the city had been severed. It was clear to me that whatever I would do next, I would do alone.

CHAPTER THIRTEEN

Okayama

I RELIED ON FRIENDS A great deal in those weeks and months after I left the hospital. I saw a lot of Teruo. I also spent time with Mitsuo, another friend of Teruo's, and his friend Hisashi. We were constantly together, our small band of young men. I was living in a room in my cousin Hideko's neighborhood, but I spent a lot of time visiting with my friends. They all had families. More than once the families of my friends stepped in to feed me and help me along.

Kunio's family had continued to operate their dagashi-ya during the final months of the war. They had picked right up again with business in the aftermath of the bomb. They were doing brisk business, buying and selling in the black market trade that was thriving in the city. The end of the war brought both chaos and change to Hiroshima and all of Japan. The steel grip of the Imperial government had loosened, and with it went the old order and control of business and economy. Black markets flourished. Networks of organized crime spread. Prices soared.

Kunio's family store was brimming with food and goods, procured and sold again along these murky pathways. Kunio's family was generous with me. They allowed me to borrow whatever I might need from their stocked shelves. They gave me food. And they included me at their table, feeding me often.

Teruo's family was also protective and watchful over me. Teruo and his mother continued to stay with his sister and her husband, as their home near the center of Hiroshima had been destroyed. I would visit them and share a meal with them. His mother fed me and worried after me in nearly equal measure. She cried when she saw me for the first time after I left the hospital, my trimmed ear still looking red and misshapen.

"Oh, Shinji!" she cried. "They've made you a mutant." She meant the Americans.

It was a strange and difficult time, with so many of us see-sawing between gazing backward in shock and horror at what had happened to us, and setting our eyes forward toward an uncertain future. I knew I had to take steps to shape my own life, to find a path that would secure me a decent future. But without a family, this would be difficult. If Takaji were home, things would be different. We could navigate this crooked new path together. Until my brother returned, I was a war-orphan, in a culture that looked down on orphans, or individuals without family references, no matter what made them that way.

Before I could open a new door to my future, there was another door that I must properly close. I had borrowed 30,000 yen (approximately 300 dollars) from a friend to cover living expenses while I looked for paying work. I took a small amount of that money and bought myself a train ticket to Okayama, to the village of Kamo, where my mother had gone to stay with her cousin. I did not expect to find her alive. Her cirrhosis must have taken her life by now. My trip was a homage to my mother's memory.

As soon as I was able, I left Hiroshima for the mountains. I needed to pay my respect for my mother's soul at the altar in her cousin's home, in the place where she was born and likely had passed.

I also needed to thank Aunty Shigeyo for caring for my mother. Not only had Aunty Shigeyo tended to my mother during the final phase of her illness but also, by giving her refuge outside the city, she had spared my mother the horror of the bomb.

When I arrived in Kamo, Aunty Shigeyo welcomed me with her usual warmth. She had tears in her eyes as she pulled me close to her. My aunt was not reluctant in showing her emotions. Shigeyo was a woman full of feeling and enthusiasm, which she could not help but share. She was impossible not to like. Shigeyo had been born the only child of her family, and grew up alongside her cousins Nami and Chiyono. The three girls had all been like sisters to each other. Aunty Shigeyo had married and had six children of her own. In the years when my family lived in Kamiyanagi-cho, all but one of her children had come to stay with us. My parents Fukuichi and Nami had helped Shigeyo's children in whatever ways they needed, from arranging a marriage to finding a job and providing them a place to live while they attended the city's excellent schools. The bond between Shigeyo and Nami had been close and devoted. Walking into her home, I felt enveloped in the warmth and security of that bond.

I had not been wrong. My mother had died, nearly two months earlier. I was not surprised. In my heart, I'd known she was dead. But I'd also ached to see her one last time. This was not to be.

Aunty Shigeyo hustled me inside. She fed me a meal. And she told me the story of my mother's final days.

When Nami arrived at Aunty Shigeyo's home, she was already very weak and in tremendous pain. She rested a great deal. But she also spent time with her extended family. She had enough strength to sit in Aunty Shigeyo's kitchen while Shigeyo's daughters worked to prepare food. Nami taught them how to cook during those days, talking them through the steps to make the meals she'd made thousands of times, but now was too weak and sick to prepare. They spent many afternoons this way, talking and laughing together.

Nami's pain was severe, but she bore it quietly. And she did not let it stop her from doing whatever simple things she could do in the time that remained for her. She missed my father, Takaji, and me, Aunty Shigeyo told me. But she did not complain.

Nami had been at Aunty Shigeyo's for a few weeks when the bombing in Hiroshima occurred. News of the bomb was broadcast on August 7 on the radio. Over crackling static, they heard this report:

> "Hiroshima suffered considerable damage as a result of an attack by a few B-29s. It is believed that a new type of bomb was used. The details are being investigated."

The broadcast contained excruciatingly little detail. The newspaper reports that circulated the next day offered little more in detail. Nami was frantic and sleepless with worry. She was desperate for information. As days passed and she heard nothing from my father or myself, she struggled to remain strong and composed. She clung to the hope that somehow we, her son and husband, had escaped the worst fate.

Those hopes were crushed in late August, when a distant cousin arrived in the village, having traveled from Hiroshima. Shuuki was another of the many relatives who had been recipients of the generosity of my parents. He had come from Okayama to Hiroshima to find work, and my father and mother had helped him. Eventually, he found a job and settled in his city. He married and bought a house of his own. He was working at the Army Second General Headquarters when the explosion occurred. Shuuki raced home to find his wife. Their home had collapsed. Shuuki's wife was inside. He could hear her screaming from underneath the debris. He pulled at the pile of rubble that had trapped her, but he was not able to release her. As the fire that raged across the city swept toward him, Shuuki was forced to make a terrible choice. He fled from the ruins of their home and from the fire that was rolling toward them, unable to free his wife in time.

Shuuki had returned to the site where his home had once been. He dug through the dust and ash-covered debris, and retrieved the charred bones of his wife. A few weeks after the bomb, Shuuki had traveled back to Okayama to bury his wife's remains in their family grave.

Shuuki also brought news for Nami. In the days after the explosion, he'd gone looking for my father and me. He'd found Fukuichi after I had been taken away by the military, still in Fuchu. After he'd seen my father, Shuuki had spoken with the brother of a friend of mine, who had told Shuuki of the extent of my injuries.

"Fukuichi may make it," Shuuki told my mother and her cousin. "But Shinji was severely burned. He won't survive."

At this point, my Aunty Shigeyo broke from her story.

"That stupid Shuuki," she hissed. "What a big mouth he has! I don't know why he couldn't have told your mother something hopeful about you. She was dying." Aunty Shigeyo shook with anger. "Thanks to him, we went through hell after that day."

The news had shaken loose the last of Nami's reserve, along with whatever shred of hope she'd carried. My mother lost her mind with grief. She had endured with fortitude the torrent of physical pain that her illness delivered. But she could not bear the agony that came with the news of my death.

"My son was killed! Oh my God, my son was killed!" she cried. Nami was inconsolable. Day and night, she lamented my death. There was nothing that Aunty Shigeyo or anyone else could do to comfort her or quiet her grief-stricken ranting. My mother also turned her anger toward my father. She railed against him for not saving my life. She castigated him for not being willing to take my place, to give his life, in a trade of fates, in order to save mine.

"My son was killed! So young, my son was killed!" Her screaming went on for days. Aunty Shigeyo shook her head as she recalled Nami's hysterical, unending grief.

And then my postcard arrived.

It was September 10. Aunty Shigeyo had been out running errands and returned home to find the mail on the floor in the foyer. When she read the message she nearly lost her head with joy. Forgetting even to take off her wooden slippers, she ran to Nami's bedside to give her the news.

"Shinji is alive! Shinji is alive!" My aunt shouted to her cousin, her feet clomping the floor in her *geta*.

To my mother, this was nothing less than a miracle at the hour of her death. She wept with joy and relief, her frail body shaking against her sobs. Aunty Shigeyo cried at her side. Together they stared at the postcard with its unfamiliar handwriting, the news of my survival that had been penned by a kind stranger. My mother had been consumed by anger and raging grief. Now, she was filled with happiness and contentment. She spent her final days this way.

It was three days later that my mother took her last breath. Nami died on September 13, which was also my brother Takaji's twenty-third birthday. My mother died in peace, knowing that I was safe.

Aunty Shigeyo beamed at me with pride. "What a dutiful son you are. You did a great thing when you sent that postcard," she told me. "You really saved your mother."

In the months since the bomb, I had felt so many things. Pain and anger, sorrow and rage, anxiety and terror and confusion. And so much of the time, I felt helpless. At last, I'd been able to do something. I'd been able to ease the suffering of the woman who had given me everything. The woman who had loved me with her whole heart.

CHAPTER FOURTEEN

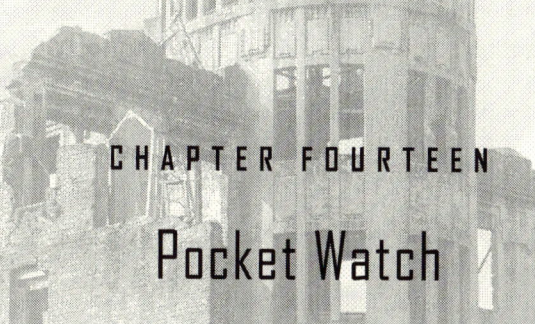

Pocket Watch

I RETURNED FROM OKAYAMA deeply comforted by the knowledge that my mother had found peace in her final days. I mourned her death. But hers was a death I had known was coming, a passing I'd been preparing to accept for some time.

My trip to Okayama had also brought me other news that I was far less prepared to accept. Aunty Shigeyo had received no word from my brother. And hearing Aunt Shigeyo recount Shuuki's visit to Fuchu to see my father thwarted the last of my hopes that somehow I might find him alive.

When Shuuki had gone looking for my father and me in the days after the bombing, he had used his contacts at the General Second Army Headquarters to locate my father at the elementary school in Fuchu. It was there that he'd found my father after the military had taken me away for treatment. When Shuuki arrived at the school, he found my father in the same gymnasium room where we'd stayed together. The conditions at the makeshift rescue center had not improved. The villagers of Fuchu were still working dutifully to care for the injured who'd made their way to them from the city. And they were continuing to do this without medical supplies, doctors, nurses, or even enough food to feed those who were well enough to eat.

Shuuki found my father weak and listless. His right arm, where he'd suffered the worst of his burns, was an ugly sight. My father's arm was blackened, oozing and carried a foul scent. Without proper cleaning and treatment, his burned flesh had begun to rot. Shuuki could see bone exposed beneath the dead flesh.

He could still speak normally. My father was so fond of words, and used them with such cutting precision, with so much insight. It did not surprise me that even as his body was failing him, his vernacular remained strong.

When Aunty Shigeyo gave me this news, I reeled. I could no longer deny the reality that had most certainly occurred; my father had died in the days or weeks that followed our separation. For all the days since we parted, I had kept hold of a narrow thread of hope, hope that somehow my father might have survived. Hearing Aunty Shigeyo's words, I realized that survival was more than unlikely.

Despite my certainty about my father's fate, I returned to Hiroshima determined to search for him. I asked everyone I knew if they had heard news or word of him. I looked to my former colleagues at the army armory for information. The truth was, I had no idea how to find him, or how I might re-trace his steps. Other than Shuuki, no one I knew had seen my father since the day I said goodbye to him.

There was only one place I knew to go. The same place my father had taken me when we had been at our most desperate.

I made my way back to Kamiyanagi-cho, to where our house had once stood. The last time I'd been there was when my father and I had staggered back to our neighborhood from the Tosho-gu Shrine. Making it back to our destroyed home in the bloody chaos of those days had been a turning point for us, launching a string of events that had saved my life.

This time, I had no such expectation of miracles.

The streets had been partially cleared, enough so that traffic could travel the thoroughfare. But debris remained in tall piles on all sides of the street. It had once been a lush and lovely place, cultivated and immaculate. Now, with the fires long since snuffed out, it was a wilderness of debris and desperation. Plants grew wild and green amid the grey ash. The family who had helped my father and me on that awful night months ago were still living in the Shimazus' storage, making due as best they could. I could see along our street that other people were encamped in makeshift shelters built from salvage, doing whatever they could to survive. I wondered if the desperation that enveloped the people of my city would ever lift. After months, I was still capable of being shocked by the devastation. Nowhere was that more true than here in the place that had once been my home.

I stood at the site where our house had been. I kicked at the debris beneath my feet. Most everything was burned beyond recognition. What hadn't been completely destroyed had been shattered into pieces. In shards of broken china, I recognized our bowls we'd used for our morning meals. Everything was covered with ash and soot. I thought of my father's professional photographs, and the photographs of our family, all burned to dust.

I moved a little deeper into the rubble. I was not looking for anything in particular. I just felt compelled to dig, to sort through the bits and pieces that were all that was left of my family's possessions. I was surprised when my hands pulled my old knapsack from the pile. The one my father had looked frantically for and couldn't find. I shook it hard to release the thick layer of soot. Beyond being filthy, it seemed only lightly damaged. I threw it over my shoulder and turned back to the deep trough of debris, now curious to see what else I might find.

It was then that a glint of something registered in the corner of my eye. High in the sky, the midday sun was bouncing off something metallic. I kneeled and used my hands to sweep away the dirt and ash, looking for the source of this reflection.

My breath stopped when I saw the round disk, caked with dirt and soot. I clasped my hand around the metal mass and lifted my father's pocket watch from the debris. I recognized our house key chained to it. I turned the watch face up. The glass had been blown off, as had the watch hands. The metal was rusted and burned. The unimaginable intense heat that reached several thousand degrees Fahrenheit from the blast had fused the shadows of the hands onto the face of the timepiece, slightly displaced, leaving distinct marks where the hands had been at the moment of the explosion. It was enough to clearly see the exact moment the watch stopped.

8:15.

My father's watch had somehow survived the explosion and the fire. It had stopped working at the very moment of the blast, forever marking that moment in time.

Standing atop the charred remains of our former lives, holding my father's broken watch in my hands, I felt as if time had stopped yet again. I remembered seeing the watch on the breakfast table that very morning. I stared at the watch, rolled it gently in my hands. I felt its weight in my palm. My father had carried this watch with him constantly. It was always at his side or in his pocket. My father's own fingers had worn to a smooth finish the rounded metal that I now cradled in mine. The watch was here. My father was gone.

I cried standing on the broken pieces of wooden posts and roof tiles, as the full force of my father's death hit me like another blast.

Our city may have been demolished, and our government may have capitulated, but there was still bureaucracy, and paperwork to make official even the deepest and most personal losses. Shortly after my visit to Kamiyanagi-cho, I went to the Prefectural Office to request a death certificate. Any survivor benefits would require such documentation of my father's death. When the official presented me with my father's certificate, my eyes went immediately to one line. The cause of my father's passing was listed as an "unnatural death," which carries a connotation of something less than honorable. Hot anger rose inside me. This banal and bureaucratic language took my breath away. My father had died as a direct consequence of the war, one of hundreds of thousands of civilians to fall victim to a conflict that had gone on for many months longer than it should have. I wanted the final comment on my father's death to speak the truth, not a vague euphemism. Denial and hubris, as much as a bomb, had contributed to the death of my father.

I could no longer wait and hope to be reunited with my father. The only hope I had left for my family lay with my brother. Soldiers were now streaming home in droves. Takaji must be among them. If not now, then soon. Not long after I'd visited the Prefectural Office for my father's death certificate, I returned to plead for information on my brother's whereabouts. They had no information on his squadron.

As grief layered upon grief, I could do nothing but wait and hope.

CHAPTER FIFTEEN

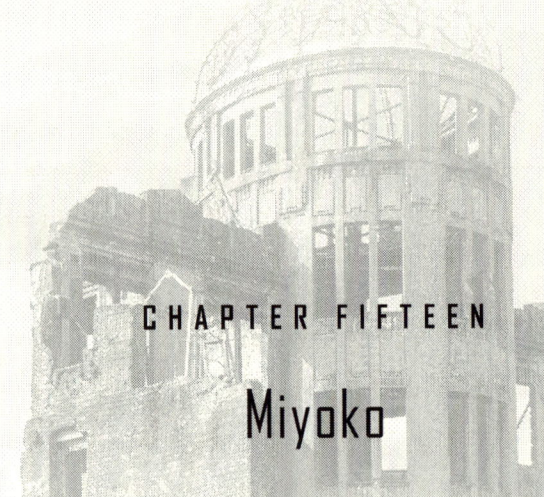

Miyoko

I GRIEVED FOR MY MOTHER and father. But grief would do nothing to change my circumstances.

I had no money and no work. People were flowing back into the city, but there was little to support them. Unemployment was raging nationwide. Food was scarce. Under the direction of the U.S. command, local and national government had undertaken the effort to rebuild the city. At this early stage, that effort was consumed by clearing the seemingly endless wreckage that remained. Rebuild to what? I wondered. Hiroshima had been a city largely defined by the military and academia. Its importance as a strategic location for the Imperial forces had been a source of pride and identity for its citizens. Its industry had been largely devoted to military production. Now, the terms of Japan's surrender included dismantling the nation's military forces and infrastructure. Whatever was to come for Hiroshima, its future would be unrecognizable from its past.

Like the city that surrounded me, my life felt in shambles. It was difficult to pick up the pieces. My situation was complicated by the fact that I was now without family. In Japan, family is currency. Family is security. Family is respect in the eyes of others. Family is the means by which others know you and place you in the world. Alone, without a family to speak on my behalf, I was nothing more than a street rat, an orphan of the war.

I wished for nothing more than to have my big brother Takaji come home. Everyday, I woke up and wondered if today would be the day that my brother strode through my door, prepared to take charge of our lives. Takaji would know what to do, how we should manage. My brother was six feet tall, an exceptionally tall and strong man for that time. He had never been shy to a challenge. Unlike me, he did not shrink when confronted with the unknown.

When the brokerage where he worked was shuttered in 1943, under the weight of Japan's collapsing wartime economy, Takaji was sent to work in a shipbuilding factory in Onomichi City. He was twenty years old at the time. With labor shortages rising as men were called to the draft, our government had passed a law forcing students and anyone younger than the draft age to fill the gaps in the workforce. Takaji had only worked in business. He was experienced at dealing with people and numbers. But he had no training in building or mechanical trades. I was his younger brother, but at the time I fretted for his success at the factory, with so little experience.

I needn't have worried.

"Oh, well, I'll wing it somehow," Takaji told me breezily, when I asked him how he would manage at the factory. And he did just that. Takaji became one of just a tiny handful of new recruits selected to work in the shipbuilding factory's office. While most others lived in cramped factory housing, my brother lived in a more spacious staff dormitory. His workday hours were shorter, and the work was less harsh. When food was scarce, he and his colleagues were eating tangerines, having pooled their money toward the purchase of a big box of the delectable sweet fruit. My brother knew how to transform a situation to his best advantage possible. His confidence was something to behold. Alone and overwhelmed, I prayed to find that confidence in myself. But mostly I prayed for my brother to come home to supplant the lack of confidence that I felt.

In the meantime, I searched for work. The army had trained me well. And I had taken to my electrical apprenticeship with all the enthusiasm that I'd once had for my studies at school. I had learned my trade. Now I must find ways to use it. With so many others looking for work, the prospect seemed daunting.

As I anxiously plotted a plan for my survival, I also had many small, practical things to do to restore some semblance of order to my life. For all of us who survived the bombing, there were a multitude of details to tend to in putting our lives back together. Among the many of these tasks before me was to restore my financial records. I had a postal savings account with some money, but the deposit record had been destroyed, along with everything else in our house. My friend Mitsuo had a sister who worked at the Postal Savings Center, and I asked him to introduce me to her, in hopes she could help me replace my deposit book and reclaim my small reserve of funds.

It was February of 1946 when Mitsuo arranged this meeting. This was not the first time his sister and I had met. A couple of years earlier I'd been at Mitsuo's house, and I'd been briefly aware of her presence. Another time I'd stopped by Mitsuo's house to deliver something for our friend Teruo. When Mitsuo met me at the front door, I could hear the clamor of young voices in the background. It was a pretty and cheerful sound, and I imagined that his sister's was among them.

But this meeting was startling and different. The first time I saw Miyoko was at the entrance to her home. At eighteen, she was a few years older than her brother Mitsuo, and just a year younger than I was. I remembered Miyoko from years before. But I did not remember her soft, round features being so pretty, or her skin so glowing. I did not remember her quiet and gentle manner as quite so sweet and appealing.

Miyoko's brother Mitsuo was a good friend. He was fun to be around, and he made me laugh. He was also prone to youthful laziness.

Brother and sister were very different. Where Mitsuo was gregarious, Miyoko was reserved. Where Mitsuo was light-hearted, Miyoko was serious. And where Mitsuo was averse to hard work, his sister was studious and diligent. Miyoko had gone to work, as I had, at the age of fourteen. She was a bookkeeper at the Postal Savings Center. It so happened that Miyoko and I had also attended the same elementary school at the same time. She was a year behind me, and I did not know her then. Miyoko was very smart and very good at math and abacus. In school, she'd been one of a very few students awarded a certificate and a special armband to wear, signifying excellence at abacus. I remembered seeing those students in the halls at school, proudly wearing their armbands. I admired them for being so smart and successful.

After that day when I first met her officially, Miyoko and I began to spend time together. I loved her soft beauty. I was impressed by her quick mind. I admired her caring heart. And with her companionship, I felt less alone.

Miyoko was from a decent, hard-working, industrious family. She was the oldest daughter among six siblings. One sibling, the first-born boy, had died as a young child. Her parents ran a home-based business in the city making tofu, labor-intensive work that required long hours. Their days started at 3 o'clock in the morning, when they rose in the dark to steam the soybeans that had soaked in water overnight. By dawn, the soybeans had cooked into tofu and the mass was cut into blocks, ready for delivery to markets around Hiroshima. The family's tofu was so delicious that people would show up at their house, mixing bowls in hand, clamoring to buy a block of the soft, silken delight for their morning miso soup.

Miyoko's parents had been working at their business since the early 1930s. In 1943 they had suspended the business when, like so many other food staples, soybeans had become impossible to obtain. But they'd quickly resumed their operation as soon as the war was over.

By 1943, Miyoko and her elder brother Toyoto were already working. Their income helped the family to make ends meet.

The bomb had not spared their family of tragedy. Two of her siblings, her oldest brother Toyoto and her younger sister Harue, had both perished in the explosion. In addition to her parents and her brother Mitsuo, her brother Iwao had survived. Iwao was eleven at the time of the bomb and had been evacuated from the city.

Miyoko had been at work on the morning of August 6. She was sitting at her desk inside the brick building that housed the Postal Savings Center at 8:15 am. She saw a flash through the window and heard a thundering boom. Miyoko did not hesitate. With lightning-quick reflexes, she did exactly as she had been trained to do in countless air-raid drills. She threw herself under her desk. She covered her eyes with her fingers and plugged her ears with her thumbs, so that her eyes would not pop out and her eardrums would not break. Miyoko stayed curled under her desk for a very long time. She could hear people screaming and moving around in the office. But Miyoko was an obedient girl. She had been told to stay still under her desk, so she did exactly that. Once, she peered out from behind her fingers. But the air was so dark and thick with dust and smoke that she could not even see her own nose. Who knows how long she might have stayed there if a co-worker hadn't seen her huddled underneath her desk.

"What are you doing?" the woman screamed. "We need to run!" The woman pulled Miyoko from her hiding place underneath her desk and pushed her toward the stream of people who were attempting to make their way out of the building. The glass windows of the building had blown apart, and many people inside had been stabbed by the flying shards. Blood was everywhere. Furniture was broken. Walls were cracked and in danger of collapsing.

Miyoko was confused and disoriented. She concentrated on following the people in front of her. Then a woman behind her screamed in her ear. "Girl," the woman shrieked at her, "you are losing your arm!"

Miyoko turned to look. Thick chunks of glass had lodged in her back, near her shoulder blade. The glass had cut through her flesh, and her arm was dangling loose from her body, as if it might come off altogether. She was in such a state of shock from the explosion, she had not realized she was injured.

Miyoko managed to make it out of the building and to a nearby riverbank where people were gathering. From there she and others fled to safer ground, eventually she made it home, which had been spared serious damage in the blast. She did not lose her arm. But without proper medical care, it healed roughly, leaving two thick bundles of scars across the upper right side of her back. She had been both lucky and very brave.

I knew that Miyoko's parents did not approve of me. I had been picking up odd jobs. But I had no steady employment, no stable job to anchor me or to support a family of my own.

Worse still, I was without a family. I was on my own, with no one to recommend me. Miyoko came from a decent family. Her father, Gunichi, had been born into an old money clan in the mountains, in the village of Shiwaguchi, about an hour north of Hiroshima. Her mother, Ochie, had also come from north of the city, born into a family in the town of Okoe. Gunichi was twenty years older than Ochie. He had several previous wives. Gunichi's family had been wealthy, but much of their assets were lost over the years. By the time Ochie's parents sent her to marry him, Gunichi was not wealthy. This meant Ochie had to work very hard throughout their married life. In addition to raising five children and keeping a home, Ochie shouldered much of the burden and the labor of their tofu business.

I could not help but see Miyoko's father in stark contrast to my own. The two men were about the same age and had come to family life in their later years. But otherwise, they were opposites. My father was forward thinking, practical and rational. He was keen to learn and flexible with his mind, open to new ideas and ways of thinking. Gunichi was none of these things. He was superstitious, irrational and narrow-minded. He was always looking to the past, mostly toward grievances. My father was a master problem solver. Gunichi threw his hands up at difficulty and chose to complain rather than negotiate a solution.

Still, they were a family. And I was an outsider, whose interest had fallen on their industrious, obedient daughter. As the months went by and Miyoko and I grew closer, I hoped that Miyoko's parents might come to view me differently. Like so many of my hopes, this one was not to be realized.

In the fall of 1947, after months of working piecemeal jobs around the city, an opportunity came to me through an old friend. Yoshio was a great friend from my days at the army armory. He was very bright, and when we were younger he had passed an exam to attend the Army Youth Telecommunications School. Yoshio had gone off to school, and Teruo was moved to his station next to mine.

Now, two years after the war had ended, Yoshio was running a mechanical shop of his own. He made me an offer to come work with him in his business. I had been picking up enough work to get by, but I was eager for more work. I wanted steady employment and an end to the uncertainty of small, itinerant jobs.

Yoshio's offer also came with a place to live. My friend suggested that I come to live with him, his wife, and his grandmother. Yoshio's grandmother was from a prominent family in Hiroshima. The arrangement was for me to work and live with them, in exchange for room, board, and a small salary. I was still living in the small room that my cousin Hideko had arranged for me. Taking Yoshio's offer meant not only steady employment, but also a more spacious and comfortable place to live.

8:15

After months of achingly slow progress, I felt my life shifting, changing for the better. I liked this feeling, and I wanted more. The prospect of a new job and a new place to live emboldened me. I took another important step forward with my life.

I asked for permission to marry Miyoko.

Her father met my request with derision. Gunichi was so affronted at the notion, he refused even to take my request seriously. Miyoko was their only living daughter. The idea that they would allow her to marry a war orphan, without any family connections, was unimaginable to them. And they let me know in no uncertain terms.

I pleaded with Miyoko's father. "I know I'm just a street rat now. I am poor, and I have no solid job. But I know I work hard." Once I had a chance to establish myself professionally, I promised, I would be able to provide a comfortable life for their daughter. I also promised to take good care of Gunichi and Ochie when they got older, as any good son would.

Gunichi laughed at me. He mocked my ambitions and my promises to him. "There is no way," he said. "I don't believe you have any chance to amount to anything. I wouldn't want you to take care of us. You couldn't do that even if you wanted to."

There was nothing left to say. Miyoko's parents would not be moved. Gunichi made very clear the consequences for his daughter should she choose to follow me out the door. Miyoko would be disowned.

I don't know if her father and mother could have imagined what happened next. Their eldest and only living daughter had always done what she was told. This was a girl who stayed perfectly still under her desk at a building threatened to collapse around her, rather than break from the rules or veer from her training.

So I could only imagine their surprise when their very compliant daughter shook her old life off her shoulders in one single act and followed a street rat out the door.

CHAPTER SIXTEEN
The Last Family Member

THE SUMMER BEFORE MIYOKO and I eloped, a telegram arrived for me.

April 10, the 20th year of Showa Era (1945).

Takaji Mikamo killed during mission on P. Island. Detail in letter.

After two years, news of my brother had arrived. It brought an end to my hope that my brother would return to me. My brother was dead. He'd died in combat nearly four months before the bombings of Hiroshima and Nagasaki and the surrender that followed shortly after.

The arrival of this news caused the most emotional pain since the bombing. My brother's survival had been my last and only hope. Hope to reclaim a portion of the family that had been lost to me. Hope to have an intrepid partner in navigating the world and its challenges. Despite the time that had gone by, I'd never stopped believing that I'd see him saunter into view, joking and laughing, to rescue me from my orphaned state.

I cried for many hours the night the telegram arrived. There seemed no end to my tears. This loss hit me harder than those that had come before. My mother was gravely ill. I'd known this, and as much as it pained me, I had accepted that she was going to die. I'd seen firsthand my father's injuries, the horrible and depraved conditions he'd faced in the days after the explosion. As strong as he was, I knew he'd faced impossible odds of surviving. My father had sacrificed what energy and life he had left in him to ensure my safety. Even before his death was confirmed, I'd understood that it was likely.

But I had never permitted myself even to think that my brother might not come back. Takaji was young and strong, full of confidence, energy, and courage. The war simply could not take him.

But it had.

The date of my brother's death haunted me. April 10, 1945. I'd been waiting for his return for two years, and he'd been dead that whole time. He'd died in those final desperate months of fighting. This was after Iwo-jima fell, and we were still pushed forward in war, despite the fact that victory was hopeless. Fighting in the Philippines had been some of the fiercest and bloodiest of any in the Pacific war. Japan had flooded the island nation with its soldiers. These forces were the final defense against an advancing enemy, and they were told to fight to the death. My brother was amongst them.

I could have wished that my brother had surrendered to the enemy. As a prisoner of war, he would likely have survived. But I knew that my brother would never have capitulated. Takaji was a leader. He was full of swagger, and his confidence was matched by his wits. He was so much like our father. Takaji would not have surrendered. Loyal and courageous, he would have been out front. It was these very admirable qualities, his courage and loyalty, that I believed must have led to his death.

Hours passed, alone in my room in Ozucho. As my gasping sobs slowly turned to quiet tears, I thought of my brother as I'd last seen him, more than four years earlier.

Takaji stood six feet tall, a head above most other men, and had passed the draft exam with an A grade in March of 1943. The army immediately sent him away for three months of training. He returned to our home in Hiroshima in June, looking fit and strong in his soldier's uniform. It was that summer that Takaji received a "Red Paper," the notice the military sent to activate a soldier's service. He was on his way to the front lines as an infantry soldier. We had no idea where he would be going. The military demanded this information be kept even from families of the soldiers.

My parents organized a celebration for my brother and his entrance into battle. These celebrations were a customary ritual for families with sons going off to war, an acknowledgement of the honor it was to fight on behalf of our Living God Emperor Hirohito. In the 1930s, during the years of Japan's war against China, these send-off celebrations were large and often ornate. Banners flew proclaiming *Congratulations for Going to the Front!*, and parades of well-wishers held Japanese flags high as they marched young soldiers to the train station. By the time Takaji was drafted, these celebrations had become much smaller and more subdued. My brother's departure was scheduled on a workday for me. I had wanted very much to stay home to see my brother off, but my father was firmly against it. Ever practical, he saw no use in my missing a day of work to celebrate my brother's activation into the military. So I went off to the army armory as usual, dejected at missing the festivities and a last, precious few hours in my brother's company. About thirty of our neighbors gathered, in formal dress, to send Takaji on his way shouting *Banzai!*, meaning "ten thousand years of prosperity for Emperor Hirohito!"

It was strange to have my brother gone from our home. As much as he'd teased me and baited me with his sarcastic humor, I missed him terribly. When I arrived home from work one evening in September, my parents told me Takaji had returned to Hiroshima. They had just returned from visiting him at the Seibi School nearby where the army was housing soldiers. Our family was not wealthy enough to afford a telephone. To reach my parents, Takaji had to call one of our neighbors.

I was anxious to see my brother, so my mother and I walked back to the Seibi School. A sign stopped us at the gate. "Visiting hours over. No visitors allowed." I was bitterly disappointed. I had arrived too late and missed what might have been my only chance to see my brother.

Just as my mother and I turned to walk back home, the soldiers guarding the school entrance changed shifts. I saw a tall soldier striding out toward the gate. It was my brother. I nearly leaped with glee.

"What are you doing here?" Takaji looked surprised and pleased to see me. We talked through the iron gate for several minutes. I noticed he was not wearing regular combat boots, but only thick socks on one foot. Takaji told me he'd had an accident during training. He'd stabbed his own foot with a knife that was attached to the tip of his rifle. I couldn't imagine my coordinated, athletic brother making such an error. Learning to be a soldier must be very difficult, I thought.

My brother was a member of the infantry. His stories of training with weapons held my attention rapt. Takaji would be carrying a machine gun, not a rifle, into battle. Rifles, he said, made you an easier target. He felt safer behind his powerful machine gun. I was fascinated by every detail he shared with me. I admired my brother's physical strength and toughness. I also marveled at his quick and clever mind.

At one point he toyed with a few coins in his hand, and I could see that they were not Japanese. It was currency from the Philippines.

I realized that this must be where Takaji was headed. My brother was not allowed to tell us where he was going. But I was sure now, this was his destination. By 1943, Japan had been occupying the nearby island nation for more than a year, putting resources into securing the territory as a bastion against the enemy forces.

This visit was my last with my brother before he was deployed. My mother, Aunty Nami, went to the East Army Drill Ground on the day that Takaji was scheduled to leave, hoping for one last look at him, even from a distance. The drill ground was ringed with barbed wire, so my mother stood and watched for Takaji, scanning the crowd of soldiers departing the school for the train that would start their journey to front lines. My mother spotted a tall, broad-shouldered soldier. She waved frantically, trying to catch his attention. At dinner that evening, my mother told us the story of seeing Takaji one last time. My father was skeptical.

"Are you sure it was him?" he asked.

"Of course it was," my mother replied. "He waved right back at me."

The next day, another phone call brought my parents to the neighbor's house. Takaji was calling to say that his departure date had been changed. The soldier that my mother had given such an enthusiastic send-off was someone else's son. Being the loving mother that she was, Nami went back to the drill ground on the day Takaji was to leave the city. She watched my brother board the train, waving to him until the locomotive coughed and spit to life, and began its roll down the tracks.

This would be the last time anyone from our family would see my brother.

We did hear from Takaji once. A few months after his deployment, near the end of 1943, a postcard arrived. It had been posted from the Philippines. Takaji said very little. His letter, like all soldiers' correspondence, would be screened by the military before being released into the post. But the card's brevity did not dampen our joy at hearing from him. We took turns reading the card. I read it many times over the months that followed, and I suspect my mother and father did as well.

In the summer of 1947, after the telegram arrived notifying me of my brother's death in battle, I went back to the Prefectural Office, this time to obtain an official death notice. The man behind the counter handed me a piece of paper.

8:15

> *To Father, Mr. Fukuichi Mikamo. You are hereby notified of the death in mission of Corporal Takaji Mikamo, the 357th infantry, the Imperial Army, who was killed by artillery in the head in Takgo, Ilocos State, Luzon Island, the Philippines.*

I wondered about the details of the official record. I thought it was likely that the army had done nothing more than guess when it labeled the cause of my brother's death as a wound to the head because he was so tall. It was a small, hollow pleasure to see that my brother had been awarded a posthumous honor for his service. Takaji had been a private in the infantry. In death, he had been promoted to the rank of corporal.

My brother's death sent me into an emotional spiral. In those days after I received the news, Miyoko was a devoted and steadfast friend and companion. Her support in my grief drew us closer. Our relationship deepened, and we were engaged a few months later.

After our elopement, Miyoko and I moved directly into Yoshio's home. We would live there with Yoshio, his wife, and grandmother. I would work there as well, helping my friend to grow his fledgling business. Miyoko and I arrived at Yoshio's in October of 1947, anxious and excited for our new lives to begin. We had great hopes for this new opportunity.

But living at Yoshio's did not go smoothly. Our troubles began almost immediately. The problems we encountered had nothing to do with my work. I liked Yoshio and enjoyed working with him. I was grateful for the chance to gain more steady employment. The problem was with the mother of Yoshio's new wife. His wife's family had been very poor. In her marriage to Yoshio, their daughter had entered a prosperous family. This was good news for her family. But rather than make her generous and grateful, this change of circumstance made Yoshio's mother-in-law difficult, demanding, and cruel. The mother-in-law did not live in the house, but she was a constant presence in the home, quickly becoming a source of great tension for both Miyoko and me. The woman constantly complained to me about us living there. She chastised us for the burden we were creating.

"My daughter is really having a hard time feeding so many adults," she scolded. "Why don't you bring your own rice?"

Two years after the war had ended, food was still scarce. Rice was being rationed by the government. In order to have our rations transferred to our new home, Miyoko and I had registered our change of address at city hall. But this made no difference to the woman, who seemed to find a cruel thrill in denying us peace and acceptance in her daughter's home. She went to great lengths, even forbidding her daughter to give Miyoko soy sauce for her meals. She was unkind to me, but she saved the worst and most senseless of her cruelty for Miyoko.

I had no choice but to confront my friend about the situation. "She is *binbo baka*," he told me. He meant that his wife's mother was stupid from being so poor. "Don't worry about her."

But I could not avoid worry. I quickly grew to regret moving to Yoshio's. I particularly regretted bringing Miyoko with me. If I had known how awful our lives would be there, I wouldn't have taken the job. I liked working with Yoshio. He was a kind man, but he was unwilling to address the situation with his wife's mother that was causing us so much misery. I desperately wanted to pack up and leave, but we had nowhere to go.

And then a solution seemed to present itself. One day on the street, Yoshio ran into a friend of his, Hiroshi. Hiroshi had worked with Yoshio at the army armory before being drafted and sent to Manchukuo, where the army had been fighting the Soviets during the war. Yoshio encountered Hiroshi just as he was returning from his army deployment, with his large military-issue backpack still slung over his back. Hiroshi had great plans to start an electrical manufacture and repair business of his own. Soon after their first encounter on the city streets, Hiroshi started trying to recruit Yoshio to join his new venture.

Hiroshi had borrowed money to build a large house with a workshop to conduct his business. Yoshio was an agreeable man, who found it difficult to say no to anyone. Before he knew what he was doing, Yoshio had agreed to join the business.

Hiroshi had an ugly reputation as an underhanded man. He was widely regarded as someone not to be trusted. Yoshio's family was vehemently opposed to the idea that Yoshio would join in a business partnership with such a man.

Yoshio was a kind person, who did not like anyone to be upset. Just as he could not bring himself to stand up to his mother-in-law in order to soothe the conflict in his home, he was frozen by the warring demands of his friend Hiroshi and his family. As I listened to my friend's dilemma, I came upon a remedy that could provide a solution for everyone.

I offered to take the job with Hiroshi myself. This would release Yoshio from his commitment to his friend, and it would free Miyoko and me from our impossible living situation. Yoshio's face lit up at my suggestion.

As difficult as life at Yoshio's had been for me, it was a thousand times harder for Miyoko. She was the target of the worst of this irrational and cruel harassment and bullying. Miyoko never complained. But despite her silence, I knew she was anxious and deeply unhappy. Everyday, she was subjected to meanness and cruelty. She was on her own, cut off from her family. She was without a home of her own. And she felt, as I did, the stress of our poverty and my lack of stable employment.

There was another reason for Miyoko's worry and for my own. My wife was pregnant. When the opportunity arose to change our living situation and take a new job, I knew I had to act quickly.

Miyoko was three months pregnant when we moved to Hiroshi's home. I was relieved to be out of Yoshio's home. I was excited at the prospect of more substantial work in my new job. I was eager to get started. I was determined to make this opportunity work.

Soon after I arrived, an important business associate of Hiroshi's took me aside. Mr. Kunimoto was well-respected, a veteran of business in the city. He looked at me kindly, and delivered to me a firm warning. In quiet and stern tones, he warned me of Hiroshi's compromised ethics and corrupt business practices.

"This is not where you should stay for long," Mr. Kunimoto cautioned me. "Learn whatever you can quickly and find another opportunity."

His words brought a cloud over my hopeful prospects for the future. My initial reaction was one of offense. Why was this man trying to discourage me? But I soon saw what he and others had worried about. Hiroshi was a devious, duplicitous man. He cut corners in his work. He negotiated unfairly with his clients and was not true to his word.

I grew increasingly anxious. Our baby was due in the spring. I could not ask Miyoko to move again. And the truth was that we had nowhere to go. The only thing to do was work hard, to make the best of our difficult situation. But as hard as I worked, I could not change the character of my boss.

In May 1948, Miyoko gave birth to a daughter. We named her Sanae, which means "early sprouts of rice" and full potential for growth. The arrival of our first child should have been a joyful, celebratory event. But my worry about work and stress about our financial situation overshadowed my joy. Hiroshi continued to behave in reprehensible ways. He refused even to pay me my wages on time or as he'd promised. I could not afford to walk away from this job. But I couldn't abide his dishonesty and corruption. My conscience told me I must leave. I lay awake night after night, wondering how I could save my new, tender family from ruin.

When the summer passed with no improvement, I made the difficult decision to leave Hiroshi and find work on my own.

This difficult decision brought another, even more difficult decision quickly in its wake. Once we left Hiroshi's we would have nowhere to live. I would need time to find work and space to conduct my business. There was only one option.

A reconciliation with Miyoko's family.

I would need to speak to Gunichi and Ochie. I must apologize to them, beg for their forgiveness, and ask them humbly to take us in. I cringed at the thought. It was difficult to let go of my pride. But for the welfare of my wife and child, I must.

My first task was to inform my underhanded employer that I would no longer work for him. Hiroshi was incensed. He screamed at me, full of fury and threats.

"I will make sure you never get any work from anyone in Hiroshima!" He hissed at me, eyes wide with rage. I wondered if I had made a mistake that would haunt me. Was it right to follow my conscience at the risk of hurting my family? I thought of what my father would have done. He was a principled man. He would leave. I knew I must do the same.

Having let go of my only source of steady employment, I next took up the task of reconciling with Miyoko's parents. Hiroshi's threats rang ominously in my ear as I made my way through the streets of the city toward Gunichi and Ochie's home. I felt miserable and disheartened. I was desperate with worry over my work. In truth, I dreaded the apology I must make to my wife's parents. I knew it was the necessary thing to do. They were our only source of hope and stability, our only chance to make a life for ourselves. It was a struggle because I knew I must make a true apology. And yet, I did not in my heart believe I had done anything wrong.

My head was hung so low as I walked that I nearly missed seeing Mr. Kunimoto, who was standing at a hot soup soba stand along the street. I stopped to greet the older man, who had tried to warn me about the dangerous business I'd gotten involved in at Hiroshi's. He'd been right about everything.

Mr. Kunimoto could see that I was distressed. He asked me what the matter was. I confessed to him my troubles. I told him what had happened with Hiroshi, how right he'd been. I confided in him how difficult it had been to work alongside him, and how I'd finally quit rather than continue to work in the service of such deceit and corruption. And I told him about how Hiroshi had threatened to block my future employment prospects.

My words had proved the man right. Yet, there was not a glimmer of gloat or satisfaction in his eyes. Instead, Mr. Kunimoto put a calming hand on my shoulder.

"I understand," he said. "Don't worry. I can get you as many orders as you want. Keep your chin up," he called to me as we parted.

My knees felt weak with relief at the thought that Mr. Kunimoto might assist me in my work. I knew he was an honest and upstanding man. Still, I almost couldn't believe that I might be so fortunate. At this point my worry was so deeply entrenched that it couldn't be loosened so easily. But I felt comforted by Mr. Kunimoto's kind words, and hopeful that he might make good on his pledge to send work my way.

This hope propelled me forward toward Miyoko's parents' home.

A true apology in Japanese culture is not just confined to words. A real apology comes deep from the soul and includes both the mind and the body. In order to fully and properly apologize and seek forgiveness, one must lower one's head. It is an act of deep contrition, a signal of one's willingness to sacrifice and to suffer pain in order to right a mistake. The deeper the bow, the deeper the apology and admittance of wrongdoing.

Standing in front of Gunichi and Ochie, I dropped my knees to the bare floor. I placed my hands in front of me and bowed deeply, lowering my head to touch the ground.

8:15

I could not sacrifice my integrity by working for Hiroshi. But I would set aside my pride to ask forgiveness from Miyoko's parents. I had lost the last of my original family. I would do all that I could to protect the new family I had created.

CHAPTER SEVENTEEN

Legacies

WE WENT TO LIVE with Gunichi and Ochie. Miyoko's parents had lost three of their six children with another one in his death bed. Two had died in the bombing, and Mitsuo died a few years later from an unidentified illness. They missed Miyoko deeply. And Sanae, our beautiful and precious baby, charmed them. Even Gunichi, who was often sour, smiled at the sight of our daughter.

In Miyoko's parents' home was a small room, just four and a half tatami mats square, which I used as a shop for my work. I was full of trepidation about how I would make a living and provide for my family working on my own. But Mr. Kunimoto kept his promise. Right away, he began to send me jobs. Before long, I was hunched over my worktable for long hours in my tiny shop, repairing and creating radios and electrical appliances. Mr. Kunimoto helped me tremendously over the years. He was diligent about directing work my way. He also introduced me to other important business leaders in the city, and encouraged them to send me projects. Through Mr. Kunimoto, I was introduced to the president of Daiichi Sangyo, an electronics and appliance manufacturing company in Hiroshima. Founded in the aftermath of the war, Daiichi was growing furiously.

The company had an abundance of work. Soon, I was receiving a regular and welcomed stream of projects from them. Eventually, I had more work than I could handle. It was rigorous and tiring, but I could finally see a stable path to a future for my family, a future of comfort and security. Each day, I rose early and stayed at my table late into the night.

The city, too, was finding its way. The first several years that followed Japan's surrender were plagued with soaring inflation, widespread unemployment, and poverty. Food shortages persisted. Many thousands of people had returned to the city, but there wasn't enough work for them. Rebuilding of the physical infrastructure of the city had begun in earnest as early as 1946, but the scope of the task, to reclaim the city from the ravages of the bomb, was vast and time consuming. The seeds of progress and transformation had been planted, but they would not bloom quickly.

In the chaos and confusion of those years, criminal enterprise blossomed in the city and in Japan at large. The *yakuza*, as these crime syndicates were known, had existed in different forms for centuries in Japan. During the war itself, organized crime had diminished, as the military monitored every aspect of civilian life. With the grasp of the military loosened, and amid the economic and political confusion of the early post-war years, the *yakuza* flourished in Hiroshima. A number of my friends sought this path. Tightly organized, with strict codes of conduct and intense stirrings of brotherhood, the city's *yakuza* were a seductive alternative to the loneliness and chaos of the post-war city. Many young men I knew and liked joined one of many gangs.

One of those men was Teruo.

My friend, who had saved my life, became a *yakuza* member. I can only imagine that Teruo, with his canny mind, boundless energy, and fearless spirit, would have quickly become a favored recruit. There's no question that he thrived in the world that he chose. Over the years, he rose to a position of great power and importance in the powerful crime networks that abounded in the decades after the war. I never saw him nor heard from him after he left Hiroshima for Tokyo. Our paths diverged and did not cross again. Still, I considered Teruo as one of my saviors. His devotion and bravery in those horrible days after the explosion saved my life. I could never think of him without tenderness and gratitude.

Not long after we moved in with Miyoko's parents, I had a visit from Uncle Torao. My favorite uncle, who had been so beloved by my mother, was just as kind and engaging as I recalled. He held Sanae in his arms and made her laugh with silly faces. He presented Miyoko and me with a generous gift, 10,000 yen (approximately 100 dollars), in honor of the birth of our child. My uncle had all the warmth and generosity of his sisters. Seeing him was wonderful and bittersweet. The visit made me miss my mother terribly.

Torao died in 1955, of stomach cancer. He was only 50 years old. I grieved the death of this good man. I was pleased over the years to be able to return the kindness that Torao showed to me, by helping his sons and grandsons.

* * * * * * *

The turn of the decade brought change and progress to our battered city, and to the nation as well.

In 1949, Hiroshima was officially designated as an International Peace Memorial City, by order of the national government. Our city, which had become synonymous with war and devastation, was to become a symbol and an instigator of peace. There were many people who did not agree with this designation, whose anger at the Americans was still fierce. Hiroshima lost 140,000 citizens already by the end of 1945 as a result of the atomic bomb, and the death toll went up to over 350,000 in the following decades to radiation diseases. There was an endless supply of anger and bitterness to be found, if one wanted to find it. But I did not.

Our city was forever changed. There could be no doubt of that. But I saw nothing good to come from holding tight to animosity, from focusing on the past instead of the future. No good would come from narrowing our eyes to the complicated and vehement disposition that had engaged so much of the world at war. These were the blinders that provoked conflict, not soothed it. I wanted to look forward. I wanted to see enemies become allies. I wanted peace. And I thought nothing better could happen to a city so ravaged by war and death than to become a city dedicated to the mission of a peaceful future.

I knew my father would have felt the same. He must have been the only survivor of the atomic bomb who laughed and sarcastically thanked the Americans for saving us the labor of dismantling our house immediately after the explosion. Who else would have had such a sense of humor under near death circumstances like that? Fukuichi, had he lived, would have embraced the new landscape of Hiroshima and its new purpose. I was so confident of this that I donated his pocket watch to the city's Peace Memorial Museum. For a long time, I'd held the watch close, thinking of my father and his bravery, feeling a part of his soul continued to exist in it. But when the time came, I was ready to let go of this only keepsake I had of my father. I wanted the watch and my father's name to be widely seen and known as a reminder of both the destruction and the heroism that were displayed that fateful August day.

By the turn of the decade, the seeds of renewal and prosperity that had been planted were beginning to bear fruit. The Korean War brought a much-needed boost to the nation's economy. Japan was no longer a vanquished and occupied foe. It was becoming a valuable and strategic ally. The occupation by the American forces ended in 1952. By 1955, the population of Hiroshima had returned to pre-war levels. There was an abundance of work flowing into my tiny shop inside Miyoko's parents' house. Miyoko and I had saved our money, using only what we needed for necessary expenses. In 1954, we bought our own home, a one-story townhouse made of wood and paper right next to Miyoko's parents. Gunichi negotiated with the owner, Mrs. Tarutani, for a good price – 210,000 yen (approximately 2,100 dollars). Miyoko and I put all of our savings into the tiny flat. Gunichi was surprised to learn I'd managed to save 100,000 yen (approximately 1,000 dollars) myself.

"Well, you didn't have to pay rent all this time, so no wonder," he said. Gunichi was a man who hung on to his past grievances. Even after many years, Gunichi could not forget that his obedient daughter had run away with a street rat.

Our new house was small, and very old. It was a humble dwelling. But it had advantages. The lot was one of the larger on the street, and the house had a small backyard, which was a welcomed luxury in the city. Most importantly, it was our own. We lived there for several years until the city bought the property to build a bridge for its expanding railway system. In 1960, we moved just one hundred yards away from Miyoko's parents' home. We were given a plot of land and constructed a home with a shop for my business.

But we were not only visited by progress during those years. Tragedy had also come our way. Several months after we moved in with Miyoko's parents, our daughter Sanae contracted polio. She was just ten months old when she was stricken. Sanae was full of energy, a buoyantly happy baby. When she became listless, we knew immediately that something was seriously wrong. Her fever spiked. She cried out even at the slightest touch. We were terrified. We were struggling, with no money set aside for doctors' visits and medical treatments for there was not yet national health insurance in Japan. We managed to scrape together what we needed to get our baby under a doctor's care. I carried Sanae to and from her many doctor's visits on my back. Miyoko and I spent many sleepless nights with her worrying about how we would manage and where the money would come from.

Sanae survived her bout with polio. But the disease left its mark. Sanae was left physically disabled. Then, in 1952, our young child was again struck by a sudden illness at the age of four, this one even more devastating. Sanae contracted encephalitis, an unknown kind of infection in her brain. For a week, her fever hovered at 105 degrees Fahrenheit (40.6 degrees Celsius). She was unconscious for the entire time. Miyoko and I were terrified. We prayed for Buddha to save this little life. When she finally woke, Sanae had a blank face. She did not even recognize her mother. She did not respond to anything. Again she was robbed of her ability. This time, the disease had caused permanent brain damage. Our bright young daughter became almost like an infant again. Sanae's mental and intellectual development had been brisk. But after her illness, she was stripped of many of the gains that she'd made as a brilliant, healthy young child. She could not speak. She could not walk.

The light of our lives had been dimmed. Miyoko and I wondered what karma was being wrought upon us. What had we done? How had we failed?

Miyoko dedicated herself to the care of our disabled daughter. Sanae did not succumb to encephalitis, but she would never fully regain the mental capacities she'd once had. The encephalitis left Sanae suffering from grand mal seizures. Her tiny body shook with violent convulsions for minutes that felt like hours. For a long time, her seizures happened nearly every day. Our lives had been fundamentally and irrevocably changed. We grieved the child we had lost, and we committed our love and care to the child who survived. Miyoko poured her love and attention into Sanae. It was a bond between mother and child that could not be swayed or broken.

For many years after the war ended, we continued to battle for survival. We were poor. I worked long hours to provide my family with basic necessities. Sanae's condition and her ongoing medical needs put a terrible strain not only on our hearts, but also on our finances. We lived through harsh winters where we went without socks to pay for Sanae's medications.

It would be thirteen years before we had another child. Akiko was born. I had been hopeful of having a son. I insisted to Miyoko that all of the clothes and decorations and supplies we gathered for our baby be blue, so sure was I that we would have a boy. But our daughter Akiko had her own ideas. When she was born, our neighbors called her a godsend because they all knew our many years of struggles before Akiko. We agreed. Akiko's name means "articulate and bright child." As we grieved the loss of Sanae's mental abilities, we put all our hopes into Akiko's healthy development.

Akiko was headstrong. She was outgoing. And she was very smart. At four years old, she passed a rigorous set of exams and was granted entrance to a very prestigious private pre-school. It was a school for the sons and daughters of the city's wealthy elite. Miyoko and I felt blessed.

When Akiko was three and a half, Miyoko gave birth to our youngest daughter, Keiko. Miyoko was thirty-eight years old when Keiko was born. In those days, this was very late in life for pregnancy and childbirth. Additionally, Keiko was four weeks overdue and had grown much bigger in Miyoko's womb. The birth was difficult beyond imagination. At one point, the doctor turned to me and told me he might only be able to save mother or child, not both.

"Which do you choose?" the doctor asked me. I hesitantly and painfully chose Miyoko. We had two other children who needed their mother. After Miyoko suffered through seventy-two hours of labor with no pain medication, our baby was born not breathing. Thankfully, the doctors were able to revive her in a matter of seconds. I nearly collapsed with relief. Despite her frightening entrance to the world, our daughter Keiko was beautiful and healthy. Her name means "blessed child." Like her sister, Keiko was very bright and showed great promise in school at an early age.

By the time our younger daughters were born, our lives were very different. The government had instituted a national health insurance system. We no longer had to worry, as we had with Sanae, about how we would care for a child who was sick. My business had grown so that I took on a handful of employees to help me with the abundant work. Japan's economy was thriving, and Hiroshima had established itself not only as a city of peace, but a powerful, productive city of manufacturing and industry.

In the late 1960s, our family moved again. I purchased a plot of land and built a comfortable home for us. Our home stood on the land that had once been the East Army Drill Ground. This ground held the ghosts of my past, but my attention was firmly on our future and the opportunities that awaited my daughters.

That is not to say we ignored the past. Akiko and Keiko grew up hearing stories of their brave grandfather Fukuichi, and their devoted grandmother Nami. They knew that my family had perished in the bomb, as had Miyoko's brother and sister. But I also spoke to them about what kind of future I wanted for them. I wanted them to live in a world of peace, a world where cultures worked to know and understand each other, a world where they would never see or know the atrocities of war. I wanted more for my daughters than to merely live in that world. I wanted them to help make that world. From the time she was young, I talked to Akiko in particular about my hopes that she would venture out into the world, beyond Hiroshima, beyond Japan, to work on behalf of peace and justice, tolerance and understanding. It was my dream for her.

* * * * * * *

Throughout our lives, Miyoko was both a traditional homemaker and a professional woman. She was the engine that made our household run. She cared for everyone: our children, her parents, her brother Iwao and his wife, the employees of my business and their families. The list of people for whom Miyoko was responsible was dizzying.

Miyoko always retained the quiet, acquiescent demeanor she'd had when I met her as an eighteen-year-old girl. But just beneath the surface of that restrained exterior was a woman of great steel. Miyoko shouldered a great deal of the work and burden of our lives, at home and in my business.

In the early days of my company, Miyoko took it upon herself to learn how to manage the finances of a small business. She'd been a bookkeeper before we married, and she had been adept at math and figures since she was a schoolgirl. As my business grew, Miyoko took over responsibility for the accounting. Even with a small business like mine, it was a big job. From bookkeeping to payroll, insurance and taxes, Miyoko handled everything involving money. I had little sense of how to manage money. I remained crafty with machines, and less so with people. More than once, I was taken in by deceit. Miyoko kept a firm and wise grip on our money, which more than once rescued us from being fleeced. She saved our profits with savvy and caution. She longed to do more with our money, to invest in markets, but she did not. In those days, investing in the stock market was considered dangerous and immoral, on par with gambling. I have no doubt that Miyoko would have done well for us in the stock market. Without her steadfast hand, keen judgment, and quick mind, my business would not have survived as long as it has.

Miyoko was careful with our finances, but she pushed limits in other ways, especially when it came to her own skills. She was always learning and pushing herself to do more. My wife was very driven, perhaps more ambitious in her own realm than I was in mine.

She had learned both western-style sewing and Japanese classical hand-sewing as a teenager. She took classes in different forms of cooking, learning to create European food and elaborate Japanese cuisine. Cooking grew to be a particular passion of hers. She would

8:15

stay up all night before New Year's to prepare our holiday meal. Miyoko also learned classical dance and singing, and the art of flower arranging. When our daughters were older and needed her less, she was constantly in one class or another, acquiring new skills and deepening others.

Miyoko also went beyond the typical pursuits of traditional Japanese women. In 1965, Miyoko learned to drive. In those days, it was rare for a woman of Miyoko's age to drive herself. But my wife was not daunted. Pregnant with Keiko, she signed herself up for a two-month driver's education class. Public transportation was accessible and affordable in Hiroshima. There was no need for Miyoko to drive herself, but she craved the independence that came with a license and wanted to be able to ferry Akiko to all of her extracurricular activities.

In the 1980s, while they were still new and intimidating to many, Miyoko learned how to use a word processor in Japanese. These devices were popular in the days before computers took the world by storm. Japanese writing is complicated, and was never suited for a typewriter. The word processor made it possible to create intricate Japanese characters. But it was not an easy machine to learn. Miyoko bought a word processor and studied hard to master this machine. She was proud of her ability to use this technology. She was especially pleased because she'd never liked her handwriting. She always felt self-conscious and embarrassed by her script. In her handwriting, she saw a lack of grace, and she believed it spoke poorly about her personality and her intellect. That is what her culture believed and taught her. With the word processor, Miyoko was able to create perfect Japanese on paper. She knew how to use this machine for many years before even her daughters had learned. She never boasted, but I think she found great satisfaction and power in her mastery of tasks considered uncommon and challenging for women in those days.

Unlike my wife, I did not adapt new technology into my work. I never learned how to type or use a computer. This was in part a practical decision. My eyesight was poor, and my eyes had become weak after being exposed to the direct flash of the atomic bomb explosion. I could not handle looking at a computer screen for very long.

Aside from a few simple machines, my shop ran with very little. My tools were a slide rule, a pencil, and a calculator. I drew blueprints by hand. Over the years, I stayed with the habits and methods that worked best for me and solved my customers' problems. My business remained competitive, but not because of the tools I used. I learned my lesson very early in my work with Hiroshi. Trust and honesty are the most important service a company can provide. Everything else flows from this. "Ten years to build trust – one moment to lose it." This is my credo. This is why my business is still successful today.

Miyoko was determined to look past limits for herself wherever she could. She wanted no limits for her daughters. Miyoko put all that she had into raising our three daughters, and caring for them and pushing them toward successful lives of their own. She sewed clothes for them, spending hours to create wardrobes full of colorful dresses and intricately woven sweaters, as well as kimono and other traditional Japanese robes. When it was clear that Akiko was bright, Miyoko ushered her into a dizzying series of classes, tutors, and lessons, all designed to prepare the young girl to meet with success in her next academic hurdle. Akiko was a natural at school, and she passed each phase of her academic career with glowing success.

When Keiko was old enough, Miyoko did the same for our youngest daughter, making sure she had every opportunity to excel.

Even though we were frugal with our money, we never passed up on an opportunity for our children because of cost: books and supplies, private lessons and tutors, classes and more classes. Their education and their opportunities were the reasons we worked so hard.

Miyoko also cared for Sanae, who was a huge source of love and joy in our household as a little girl. And yet, as our eldest daughter grew older, she became more challenging for Miyoko to care for and manage. Sanae lived with us into adulthood, and continued to live with us at times as an adult until we found the right facility for her long-term care. It was difficult for Miyoko to let her daughter go, to let others care for and protect her. Miyoko believed that Sanae was her responsibility alone. Attitudes in Japan among people of our generation encouraged this belief. In a culture where sameness is valued above almost all else, there is little room for difference or special needs. Believing in karma, most families felt shame for their disabled children. They tried to hide them when possible. Asking for help, for what might be construed as special treatment, was not easy for me or for my wife. Children and adults with disabilities were seen as burdens on able people. It would be a long time before Japanese society would be able to celebrate individual differences and promote support of various needs equally. At that time in history, the parents of disabled children often felt very apologetic to the general public for burdening them or inconveniencing them. We certainly did.

The bond that existed between mother and daughter at times made things harder. Sanae trusted Miyoko like no one else. This trust sustained Sanae, and helped her grow and thrive despite her disability. But this deep bond also meant that Sanae felt free to show her emotions to Miyoko as she would never with anyone else. With me, my daughter was formal and proper, always obedient and restrained. With her sisters, Sanae was loving and caring, full of kindness. With the outside world, Sanae was friendly and open. But with her mother, Sanae could be defiant and obstinate. To her mother, she would wail and cry like a baby when she was displeased. Sanae could be demanding of Miyoko, taunting and provoking her to frustration and tears. She was at times physically out of control.

Miyoko bore the strain of this as she bore everything in her life, silently and stoically. She carried enormous responsibility on her shoulders. She woke early. She often stayed up late, sometimes forgoing sleep altogether. And in between, she rarely stopped tending to others.

For many years, Miyoko had Ochie to help her. Ochie came to our house every day for several hours, to help Miyoko with household tasks like laundry and preparing ingredients for cooking. Like Miyoko, Ochie continued to work hard her entire life. Gunichi's health deteriorated in the years after the war. By the 1960s, Gunichi was bedridden. When Akiko was a child, she would visit her grandparents' home. She would sit at her grandfather's bedside on tatami mats as he reached into a drawer in an old wooden cabinet nearby. From the drawer, Gunichi would pull a sack of coins and drop a few in his granddaughter's hand. As he had been with Sanae, Gunichi was softened by his granddaughter.

In addition to working in the business, Ochie tended to her ailing husband, and to her son Iwao and his wife. Mitsuo had died at twenty-three. Iwao was Ochie and Gunichi's only other living child. He worked with his mother in the tofu business.

Iwao and his wife Yoriko also came to work for me. Over the years, I was able to make good on my promise to Miyoko's parents, to care for them and their family. The success and growth of my business made me able to help support Ochie and Gunichi, as well as Iwao and his wife. When they stopped the tofu-making business, Miyoko and I helped them to build a four-story building on the small plot of land where the old wood and paper house was. This gave them a place to live and income from rent. In her later years, Ochie thanked me for the help I provided to her and her family. I was proud to be able to take care of my extended family as I had dreamed of doing.

Ochie lived to be ninety-four. In her final years, she developed dementia. Miyoko was a devoted caretaker to her mother. When Ochie died, the loss hit her daughter very hard. The death of her mother cracked the hard, quiet shell that Miyoko for so long had presented to the world, and even to her family. She cried out for her mother as the casket was brought past her on its way to be cremated.

"Mother!" Miyoko screamed. She nearly threw herself on the coffin. She had lost any sense of her life. In that moment, she was a child desperate for her mother, unwilling to part from her. Miyoko was strong. It took several people to pull her away from Ochie's casket.

Miyoko was seventy at the time of her mother's death. She lived for ten more years. But she never completely recovered from losing Ochie.

* * * * * * *

We moved forward with our lives after the war. The city was rebuilt around us, but echoes of the past were everywhere. Both Miyoko and I carried deep scars, intimate reminders of our ordeal. The rebuilding of Hiroshima took decades, and for all those years the physical state of the city was a constant reminder of what had occurred.

I faced other health problems. The Americans established the Atomic Bomb Casualty Commission in 1946. Their purpose was to investigate the long-term effects of the atomic bomb on our population. Survivors of the bomb were invited to an annual physical exam. Many people were skeptical and wary of this endeavor. They were afraid of the ABCC, and would not consider cooperating with the Americans.

They nuked us. And now they want to use us as guinea pigs? Without even paying us? They have the audacity to ask for our cooperation? Give me a break! Many were against it.

I saw nothing to fear. When the postcard arrived with a reminder of my checkup, I went. Our neighbors thought I was crazy.

It was in 1954, at the ABCC exam, that I was diagnosed with tuberculosis. Tuberculosis had been a scourge in Japan for decades before the war. It was an epidemic brought on by the deprivation and poor working conditions of so many of the country's poverty-dwelling citizens. Long hours, insufficient and unbalanced diet, polluted streets and unsanitary living conditions made the disease spread with lethal ease. Women were especially vulnerable. My birth mother, Chiyono, died from tuberculosis when she was only 27 years old. Tuberculosis was a frightening, mysterious disease that struck and killed with little recourse. It was an epidemic that the imperial government had largely ignored.

After the war, the government finally woke to the problem, and started to pay more attention to treatment of tuberculosis. But in 1954, we were still struggling financially. Sanae's medical crises had taken whatever meager savings we had.

The ABCC offered survivors check-ups, but no treatment. For that, I went to the Makidono Clinic. In an exam room, I was taking off my shirt when a man about my age walked in the door. It took me a moment to recognize this man as Dr. Teshima's son. Dr. Teshima, who had lived nearby to us in Kamiyanagi-cho, had been our family doctor. His son had been just one year behind me in elementary school. Dr. Teshima's son had become a doctor like his father. When he heard about my illness, he offered his help. He suggested that he treat me himself, using the latest medicines, powerful antibiotics that had recently become available in Japan for the first time. After the war ended, Japan had begun to import these drugs from the United States. But they were very expensive. Dr. Teshima offered to charge me only what it would cost him to procure the dosages.

Everyday for three months, I was injected with the powerful antibiotic that knocked out the dangerous, deadly infection. By Dr. Teshima's orders, I worked only half days, and rested for the other half. It was only because of his generosity that I was able to reduce my workload, stay afloat, and afford the medication that I couldn't have otherwise. It seemed I was still being visited by angels. I knew my father would have agreed.

* * * * * * * *

In my daughters, I saw not only the future but also the past. In them, I saw my own love of school and learning. It gave me great

8:15

pleasure and satisfaction to see the fruits of my work translate into opportunities for my children – opportunities that I did not have.

I also saw in my daughters echoes of my brother and myself as children. As she grew, Akiko reminded me so much of Takaji. Like him, she was strong-willed and full of energy. She leaped into unfamiliar territory, eager to experience new things. Akiko had Takaji's sense of humor. In her, I saw my brother's wit and playfulness brought to life again. My daughter had a mischievous streak that ran deep.

In my youngest daughter, I saw so much of myself. Keiko was timid and quiet. She lingered in the background, letting her more assertive sister grab the spotlight. Keiko cried easily, as I had. She was a sensitive child, and I recognized in her tenderness and insecurity some shadow of my own.

In their relationship, I saw echoes of the way my brother and I were together, sometimes with eerie similarity. When Akiko was eight years old, she brought home a science magazine from her classroom. She loved this magazine, which was full of experiments and project kits for children to try. This was just the sort of thing that captured the attention of my intellectually curious daughter. In this particular issue were plans and a kit for a telescope. Akiko could barely wait to get home and tear into the instructions for creating the device. By nightfall, she was peering at the stars using her new, self-made telescope.

The next night, Keiko approached her older sister, brimming with worry.

"Something spooky is happening," Keiko whispered to Akiko. "I am so scared. I think there's something creepy outside under the window in my bedroom."

Keiko begged Akiko to come look. Akiko was scared herself but slowly stuck her head out the window and gazed down into the moonlight darkness below. At first she saw nothing out of the ordinary. As her eyes adjusted to the dim light, she saw the source of her sister's fear. It was her telescope, in pieces on the ground. Akiko was relieved that it was not a monster and forgot to get mad at Keiko.

Keiko had been desperate to try the device for herself, but she was afraid to ask her sister for permission. Akiko bullied Keiko, as Takaji had bullied me. But the lure of the toy proved irresistible. So she took the telescope and attempted to use it on her own, with disastrous results. At just four, Keiko was too short to balance the telescope properly. It wobbled in her hands and dropped out the window to the ground below. Keiko was left with a dilemma almost identical to one her uncle had faced so many years before, when he held my wooden airplane in his hands. She couldn't bring herself to confess to her sister. But Keiko also knew that she couldn't pretend to know nothing of the telescope's fate when her sister inevitably came looking for it. So, like Takaji had with me, Keiko had crafted a plan to confess, while also insulating herself from punishment.

When Akiko told me this story, I laughed until my ribs grew sore. It was the very incident between my brother and me, which I'd never forgotten, now playing out again between my two daughters. I thought of how Takaji would have loved this story, the roar that his laughter would have taken. I missed my brother even more after I became a parent. I knew he would have been such a lively and devoted uncle to my children, so full of spirit and fun. I imagined they would have loved him as I loved Torao. I could see my brother lifting the little girls high over his head, and my heart ached with his absence.

Those small girls, Akiko and Keiko, grew before my eyes to become accomplished women. Keiko attended medical school at Hiroshima University and went into practice as an internist in the city. As I'd hoped, Akiko sought a life beyond Japan and a career that is devoted to promoting peace across cultures. After completing her university studies, she traveled to the United States to pursue her doctorate in psychology and started her own practice in California as a multicultural psychologist. She co-founded San Diego - WISH:

Worldwide Initiative to Safeguard Humanity, a nonprofit organization for peace and humanity promotion and education. Both my daughters became mothers themselves. Akiko and Keiko were inspired by their sister, Sanae, to devote their lives to healing. Their successes and the depth of their caring for others have made me very proud.

* * * * * * *

I never stopped missing my family. I thought of my mother, my brother, and my father often. Little things would remind me of them. A favorite piece of music of my mother's would bring her face to the front of my mind. Putting long hours in my workshop, day after day, I thought of my father in his darkroom in our house, laboring over his photographs. I thought of my brother when I watched my daughters squabble then fall to the ground in laughter.

There were times when the echoes of the past became something louder and more insistent, forcing memories of the war and its devastating climax more directly and sharply to mind.

There were two soldiers who came home from the war decades after it ended. Both men had lived in a state of solitary warfare. Their return to Japan created a sensation.

Shoichi Yokoi had been a corporal in the infantry, deployed to fight on the island of Guam. Unaware of the surrender in 1945, Yokoi spent the next twenty-seven years living alone in the jungle, waging a lonely guard against an enemy that no longer existed. A staunch believer in gyokusai, the honorable suicide, Yokoi was determined to die fighting rather than surrender to the enemies. He had sworn an oath to fight to the death in honor of Emperor Hirohito. He would not go back to Japan alive. For twenty-seven years, Yokoi lived in an underground cave. In 1972, two fishermen found Yokoi near a riverbank. When the soldier arrived back to Japan, to great fanfare, he still carried the shame of surrender.

"It is with much embarrassment, but I have returned," he announced at the airport.

Two years later, another soldier who'd refused to give up the fight also returned to a very different Japan. Hiroo Onoda had been an intelligence officer in the Imperial Army, stationed in the Philippines. Like Yokoi, word of his country's surrender and disarmament never reached Onoda. Along with three other officers, the soldier continued to execute his mission, to gather intelligence on the enemy. Over the years, the small band of soldiers conducted guerilla attacks and fought with local police. Two of Onoda's companions were killed. A third surrendered. But Onoda refused to drop his arms, or his battle stance. In 1974, Onoda's former commanding officer flew to the Philippines to relieve his soldier from duty. Onoda's one-time military superior had long since traded his uniform for a civilian life as a bookseller. He accompanied Japanese authorities back to Lubang Island to conduct the ceremony to deliver the order, so that Onoda would at last disarm.

These episodes created a flurry of media attention and discussion in Japan. Both men became celebrities. While I had tremendous respect for the strength of these men to survive, I shuddered at their stories. To me, these men were a reminder of the intense discipline based on honor that the Imperial government had so successfully waged on its own people. These men represented the most extreme result of that mentality. But it was something that we all experienced. Even men like my father, who was strong-minded and independent. And especially young men like my brother, who was full of loyalty and energy for a cause.

Both had lost their lives as a result of the prolonged and devastating war, which we'd had no choice but to support and promote despite whatever unconscious doubt existed in our minds and hearts. Looking back, there had been a particular senselessness to the last several months of that war. During that time, defeat was certain, but pride and denial pushed us to continue. In the interim, my brother and father died. I could never forget this.

* * * * * * *

Just as I had done, Miyoko also participated in the annual physicals for survivors of the bomb. Each year, she received the postcard and would dutifully attend. One August when Miyoko was in her early seventies, she went for her annual exam. There was a bus for x-ray parked outside the elementary school, where physical checkups were conducted. Miyoko had been given the option to have a chest x-ray, but she did not want to. She was exceptionally modest and prone to embarrassment. She did not want to expose her bare chest in front of the doctors and technicians, all of whom were male.

As Miyoko was leaving the elementary school, she saw one of the technicians leaning against the outside of the x-ray bus. The man looked bored. He yawned and rolled his eyes. Miyoko felt a rush of guilt.

These men are here to help people, she thought to herself. She felt sorry that no one was taking advantage of the service they were there to provide. She decided to have the chest x-ray. Her impulse to help these men feel useful was stronger than her deep self-consciousness.

This was a very fortuitous impulse. The chest x-ray found cancer in Miyoko's lungs. But because they'd found it so early, doctors were able to remove the cancer completely with surgery, and Miyoko recovered.

Miyoko had kept up the grueling pace of her life, working for the business and shouldering responsibilities at home and for her family. But after Ochie died, she struggled. In her seventies, Miyoko's mental and physical health suffered. She suffered from depressed mood and worsening memory problems. She was determined to keep doing everything she'd always done. But I made the difficult decision to give the accounting and financial work of my business to someone else. Another woman might have welcomed the opportunity to relax, and let go of responsibilities. Not Miyoko. As stressful as the work of managing the business had been for her, it gave her a deep feeling of power and purpose. Without the work, she felt frustrated and sidelined from her own life.

Relieving her of the stress of financial responsibilities did not slow her mental decline. Often, from deep inside her malaise and confusion, Miyoko would fret about the tasks she'd once had in her work with the business.

"I'm so behind on the accounting," she would say, over and over again. "I have to work. I have to catch up." These rudderless anxieties continued for days at a time.

Miyoko had stayed in touch with a few friends from her girlhood, other survivors of the atomic bomb. They were friends from the Postal Savings Center, where she was working when we met. Even after her memory problems had her deep in its grasp, she continued to think of these friends. One of Miyoko's old friends was a woman who was living in a nursing home. This friend's son had married a young woman whom his mother did not like. The mother and the daughter-in-law fought bitterly. Miyoko's friend had expected her son to care for her in her old age. Unfortunately, her son chose his wife instead of his mother and the older woman wound up living alone, full of bitterness and loneliness.

Miyoko's heart ached for her friend. She could not imagine the sadness of the woman's solitary life. Well into the stages of her own decline, she went to visit her old friend in the nursing home. Miyoko comforted her and reminded her of happier days when they'd been young. It was amazing to see how lucid Miyoko could become when there was someone who needed her care and assistance. She had always put others before herself. This never stopped, even after her afflictions took away so much of her sense of self.

Miyoko's kindness for others remained strong throughout her late years. And as she grew frailer, other feelings surfaced for the first time. She was often emotional. A lifetime of quiet rectitude, during which she'd shouldered great trauma, loss, and responsibilities, had taken its toll inside her. Now, her cognitive decline had broken her repression, and a lifetime of long-buried feelings came cascading out.

Sanae was a great worry to Miyoko in those days. It did not matter that Sanae was happy and settled in her life, living in a residential facility for the disabled, with a job, friends for companionship, and a loving family looking out for her. Miyoko could no longer see the happiness that surrounded Sanae. As her mother, Miyoko could not imagine that anyone could truly love and care for her daughter as she had. She was terrified and distraught at the thought of leaving her disabled eldest daughter alone in the world without her.

"I wish I could just take Sanae with me to *the other world.*" Miyoko would wail. Of all of her responsibilities, Sanae was the one that Miyoko could least bear letting go. Sanae had been born in a time in Japan when there was little understanding and acceptance for the disabled. But it was changing slowly. And for Miyoko, it could never have changed enough.

It was agonizing to see Miyoko live this way. She had always been so capable and in control. Her physical and mental pain was excruciating. After so many years of mental and physical decline, the disease that claimed her life was almost merciful in its swiftness.

Miyoko had attended her annual survivor's physical, again, at age 80. Her x-ray revealed a shadow on her lung. It was a different form of lung cancer than what she'd had years before, and much more aggressive. My wife died within four weeks of her diagnosis. The love I had for Miyoko and the true depths of our connection was beyond my full understanding until after she left me.

* * * * * * * *

There was also the matter of the pocket watch. In 1985, Hiroshima city officials contacted me. They wanted to send my father's pocket watch to the United Nations Headquarters in New York City. The U.N. was creating a special exhibit to commemorate the fortieth anniversary of the bombings of Hiroshima and Nagasaki. They wanted my father's watch to be part of this permanent exhibit. I was happy to give my consent. I thought of all the people around the world who might see the watch and learn from it. For years, it gave me great pleasure to think of my father's watch, proudly displayed as a symbol and a remembrance of that day.

In 1989, Akiko left Japan to continue her doctoral studies in the U.S.. She stayed in New York City for a few weeks after arriving in the U.S.. At her first opportunity, Akiko went immediately to the United Nations Headquarters in Manhattan to see her grandfather's watch. But it was no longer there. The watch had been stolen, but no one at the U.N. seemed to have been concerned. They had conducted no investigation into the theft, and Hiroshima City officials had not been notified that the pocket watch had gone missing. The most that U.N. staff could tell her was that the watch seemed to have been stolen sometime within two weeks of her visit. They knew this only because a tour guide, who had begun working two weeks before she got there, remembered seeing the watch on display, locked inside a heavy glass case.

When Akiko called me, her anger vibrated through the telephone. I was shocked to hear the news and saddened. That watch was the only tangible possession that connected me to my father. That watch, I believed, had carried part of his soul. I did not understand how the people at the U.N. could have done nothing about the disappearance.

Akiko begged me to do something to address the situation. She would attempt to get in touch with media outlets in the U.S. herself. My daughter was principled and headstrong. She saw a wrong and she intended to make it right. I understood her fire, and yet I knew that anger was not the answer. I could almost feel my father nodding alongside me as I spoke to my child, calming her down.

"Akiko, don't hate them," I said. "It's easy to blame somebody when you suffer a significant loss." The watch had been special. I could not deny this. But even so, it was only an object. The object may be gone, I told her, but the spirit behind it is here. And I cautioned her against losing hope.

"When you lose something," I said, "you will gain something." I kept my word to my child and called one of the officials of Hiroshima City. They in turn sent a communication to the U.N. But the watch was never found.

I will admit that I struggled myself to make peace with the disappearance of my father's pocket watch. There were moments when I had to remind myself of the advice I'd given to my daughter. The watch was all that I had left to connect me to my father and to our family.

Not long after I learned about the theft of the pocket watch, I dreamed of my father. It was a dream so vivid and so clear, that I recalled every word, every instant. In my dream, my father smiled at me.

"Shinji," he said. "Don't get angry. Don't get discouraged."

"There's no crying over spilled milk, is there?" My father laughed his remarkable laugh.

"I had to leave you when I was 63 years old. And now my pocket watch has left you when you are 63 years old. It's just another milestone of our lives."

My father continued, speaking words I felt in my bones were the truth. "Nothing ended that morning at 8:15 a.m. Nothing ends with my watch's disappearance."

"Life goes on. Our ties to each other, our wishes, our spirits. It all goes on. Your daughters will carry them on for both of us."

As usual, my very wise father was right.

The media in Japan picked up the story of the missing pocket watch. All across the country people heard about the disappearance of the watch that had occurred halfway across the world. They also heard about my father, Fukuichi Mikamo, and his acts of bravery and strength in saving my life. I was interviewed by television reporters and newspaper journalists. My picture, and our family story, was broadcast all over Japan.

I began to hear from distant relatives I had never known. Mikamos from all over the country wrote letters to me, tracing our legacy, looking for a connection in our past. This information helped me reconstruct my family tree. Eventually I was able to trace my ancestry on my father's side back fifteen generations, to the 1400s, when our forebears had lived as feudal lords in the Chugoku Mountains. It was just as my father had told me. But now I had proof, even after all of our photographs and documents had been burned to ashes and lost forever.

For the first time since the war, I was no longer a street rat, an orphan without family connections.

Friends of my father's also reached out. They also provided me with information about my family history. Some visited and recounted family stories I'd forgotten or had never been told. Some sent photographs of my family. Since I'd lost every single picture of my family in the explosion, each new photograph I received was precious to me. Each one was like getting back a small piece of the family I had lost. Getting the pocket watch stolen turned out to be a blessing.

Amongst the friends who reached out was the son of my father's former boss, the owner of the Kobayakawa Photo Studio in Hiroshima. This was where my father had worked in the years before the war. Mr. Suzuki and I became friends. He had been a boy when my father worked for his father. He remembered my father well.

"He was so good at making things, and he taught me a lot," Mr. Suzuki told me. My father had so impressed the boy with his technical skill and creativity that he inspired Mr. Suzuki to become an engineer.

In one of our talks, Mr. Suzuki recalled an outing with my father to the Gosasozan Mountains. A young Mr. Suzuki clambered up the path, running at a breakneck pace. My father, walking at a calm pace behind him, called out to him.

"Mr. Mikamo told me, 'Don't run at the beginning. You have to preserve your strength for the entire way.'" Mr. Suzuki told me he kept those words as a lesson for his entire life.

That was my father. He was a dreamer and a planner, a practical man and a principled one, a man of great skill and great wit. But above all, he was a teacher. I have tried to keep my father's lessons, and to pass them on to my children. I shared with them the wisdom I received from the man who gave me life, and then saved my life. Who taught me to question, and also to forgive. Who showed me what perseverance is. Who helped me to preserve my strength the entire way.

AFTERWORD

I WAS BORN IN HIROSHIMA many years after World War II ended. Growing up in Hiroshima as a child, it was hard to imagine an atomic bomb explosion had annihilated the entire city in my family's life time. The Hiroshima I grew up in was a Hiroshima of thriving culture, commerce, and education, not one of destruction, grief, and death. Nevertheless, the survivors' and victims' stories were very closeto me. I grew up listening to my father's stories, how he managed to survive the direct exposure to the heat, blast, and radiation of the bomb, and how my grandfather remained tenacious in his efforts to keep my father alive. I also heard about my aunt and uncle on my mother's side, who perished in the explosion. My mother didn't speak much of her experiences of the bombing as she was a very traditional Japanese woman who learned to swallow her pain so as not to burden others. But the deep scars on her back from the broken glass that had nearly dismembered her spoke for themselves. So did my father's missing ear lobe and the extensive burns on the right side of his body. Their wounds were visual reminders of the pain and suffering they had endured many years ago.

Learning about the atomic bomb was a perpetual part of my education growing up. Every summer as a homework assignment, we had a social studies workbook that covered the atomic bomb and Hiroshima's mission for nuclear peace. In preschool, I learned about Sadako Sasaki, a well-known girl depicted in Eleanor Coerr's true story, *Sadako and the Thousand Paper Cranes*, who was two years old when the atomic bomb exploded in Hiroshima. She developed leukemia nine years after the atomic bomb and folded 1,000 paper cranes in the hospital, in order to make a single wish for her recovery. Sadly, she died nine months later when she was 12 years old, not too long before I was born. In her memory and the memory of tens of thousands of others, we folded thousands of paper cranes each year, making a wish for peace and humanity.

When I was in the 2nd grade, our class took a field trip to the Hiroshima Peace Memorial Museum. There, I saw my grandfather's pocket watch displayed in a glass case. The watch's glass cover and both hands had been blasted off, but the heat-fused face showed 8:15, the time of the atomic bomb explosion. My father had always told me how my grandfather was a courageous man — well-respected and extremely wise. He kept instilling a fighting spirit in my father, so my father could persevere through numerous occasions where he wanted to succumb to death. My grandfather died shortly thereafter, but it was because of him that my father miraculously survived. A few months later, my father had found my grandfather's watch in the ashes where their house used to be. He kept it as the only keepsake of his father and later donated it to the Hiroshima Peace Memorial Museum. I had never met my grandparents on my father's side as they had both died in 1945, but I felt closer to my grandfather when I saw the pocket watch in the display.

My father is a liberal man for his generation and cultural upbringing, and he raised me saying, "Akiko, it's wrong to hate Americans. Yes, they bombed us, but the Americans are not to blame. You have to see the bigger picture of what was happening in the world at that time. It's the war to be blamed. I want you to grow up, learn English and learn about other cultures, and become a bridge across oceans to help people from different backgrounds with different beliefs understand one another, so no one will ever suffer from a nuclear bombing again. Contribute to society and contribute to world peace."

It was as a result of these words that I learned English and decided to move to America to study multicultural psychology. When I arrived in New York City at the age of 27, I immediately visited the U.N. Headquarters and learned of the disappearance of my grandfather's pocket watch. I was immediately filled with feelings of rage and betrayal. *How could they have been so careless? Did they not appreciate that this was the sole remaining belonging of my late grandfather? Did they feel it wasn't important enough to even have the courtesy to investigate and notify Hiroshima City and my family?* I immediately called my father to convey to him the atrocity.

My father was shocked and dismayed at the news. But he told me not to be angry. The pocket watch was merely a belonging. Its disappearance did not signify a lost connection to our family's history. It did not mean that my father and grandfather's story could not be shared with the world. The pocket watch was just an object, its symbolism and meaning were created by us, it did not intrinsically carry them.

My father taught me, once again, how we as human beings have a choice to react to seemingly negative experiences with compassion and forgiveness. I could choose to foster feelings of anger and resentment, or I could choose to be grateful that my father had found my grandfather's pocket watch intact amidst all the rubble, that tens of thousands of people were able to view it and experience a piece of our family's history, even, that somebody had valued my grandfather's pocket watch so much, that they felt the need to take it for themselves. Though our mind may elect to count the ways we have been wronged, to paint a situation in terms of "me" versus "them," it is our higher human nature that gives us the ability to turn an opportunity to hate into an opportunity to love.

Through all his pain and suffering, the loss of his family, the hardships of rebuilding his life from nothing, my father never held a grudge against the Americans for dropping the atomic bomb. He even told me how he acknowledges Colonel Paul Tibbets, the commander and pilot of the Enola Gay (who named the B-29 that dropped the atomic bomb in Hiroshima after his mother), not for dropping the bomb that killed over 350,000 people, but for accomplishing his given mission dutifully and effectively. "He was a competent military officer and pilot. He followed his order and accomplished his mission. He was risking his own life, too." My father would say.

I remember one of my psychodynamic psychotherapy professors at the California School of Professional Psychology, San Diego (now Alliant International University), teaching us the difference between sympathy and empathy from a psychological perspective. She said, "Sympathy is when you feel the same or similar emotions with the person you feel sympathy for. If she is sad, you imagine yourself in her shoes, and you feel sad with her or for her. Empathy is different. You can empathize with people without feeling the same feelings or agreeing with their views. You could even have a completely opposing opinion or feel opposite emotions and still empathize with somebody. Empathy is when you put aside your own subjective experiences and see things from the other person's perspective, considering their upbringing, culture, and personality to understand how that person might feel, think, and see. Empathy is the essence of providing psychotherapy." She gave an extreme example of empathy. She was Jewish, an offspring of Holocaust survivors. She said, "A Holocaust survivor could empathize with Rudolf Hoess, the SS Commander of Auschwitz, even if she doesn't agree with what he did and has very deep-seated feelings about it. She may empathize with the pressures Rudolf Hoess was under, the environment he was operating within, and understand why he did the things he did."

My father chose to empathize with the Americans, to understand the context and environment they were in that led to the dropping of the atomic bomb. He chose to use this experience as an opportunity to better understand human behavior, rather than to remain a victim to lifelong chains of anger, judgment, and detachment. Although, that doesn't mean he agrees with the justification of using nuclear weapons.

It doesn't take a disaster like the Holocaust or the atomic bomb to realize the magnitude of empathy. When I provide couples therapy or family therapy, I make sure to explain what empathy truly is and help my clients regain or develop it. I have seen sentiments of war in what had once been deep, loving relationships. I see this especially when couples are going through divorce, and feelings of hurt and resentment take over their otherwise intact judgment. Parents unintentionally use their children as a means to make their spouse suffer. Children suffer the most, even though these parents love them and don't intend to hurt them. But they cannot put aside their negative emotions and access their empathy within them for their spouse and even for their own children.

When you feel hurt by someone, do you wish that person to suffer as if their suffering would relieve your pain and help you to recover? It might feel in that moment that what goes around comes around, and justice should be served. But the truth is any feelings of relief or satisfaction are superficial and will not bring you peace. Empathy and forgiveness are the only pathways to true healing. Empathy provides you with a different perspective – one that can be surprisingly empowering and liberating. When you don't hold on and ruminate about how unfair something is, how badly you were treated, or how hurt you are, you allow yourself room and energy to grow and heal.

Most aggression is a reaction to fear. People strike out physically or emotionally when they fear or experience scarcity, deprivation, abandonment, attack, degradation, or loss of many kinds including independence. It's natural human instinct. But we don't have to react that way as spiritually and emotionally developed human beings.

Psychoimmunological research has shown that amongst all the negative emotions, resentment (not just anger, sadness, or other negative emotions) is found to reduce immune hormones' activities and actually make people sick. Forgiveness has been found to lead to the enhanced activation of neurotransmitters to make a person feel good and reverse the signs of depression.

I have been based in San Diego, California, and working to help people of various nationalities understand themselves and one another for growth in my own practice and consulting business as a medical and consulting psychologist and executive coach. My mission is to educate people and help them develop empathy and the ability to look at things from multiple perspectives, even in conflicts, so that they can effectively communicate and collaborate with one another. In 2011, we formed a non-profit organization, "San Diego-WISH: Worldwide Initiative to Safeguard Humanity" (www.sdwish.org). We started International Peace & Humanity Day, an annual tradition of celebrating the freedom from nuclear wars since 1945 and promoting peace and humanity on Hiroshima Day (August 6), and sending out wishes for world peace by floating paper lanterns on Nagasaki Day (August 9). Through this grass-root movement, our mission is to spread this wish for peace & humanity to the world and to educate the future generation.

This is a story of many lives I have wanted to tell for decades. I feel the time has come to share the lessons I have learned from my family, and the insights I have gained while working to help people. My mother passed away a decade ago. My father is 93 years old and still robust in Hiroshima City. He is one of the very few survivors of the atomic bomb within such fatal proximity. One could say that it is a miracle that my sisters and I exist in this world, and our children after us. I believe that it is my purpose to tell my family's story so that people may see that despite a war which caused immeasurable pain and agony to two opposing countries, these two countries can now work together and live peacefully in harmony. The U.S. and Japan were arch-nemeses during World War II, but they are now resilient allies. After the earthquake and tsunami on March 11, 2011 that killed more than 20,000 Japanese, the U.S. launched Operation Tomodachi (*"Friends"*) which was the single largest humanitarian relief effort in American history.

My wish is that people may read this story, relate to the universal notions of forgiveness and empathy, and find a means to apply it in their own lives. With the right intentions, yesterday's enemies can become tomorrow's best friends. That is my vision for the world.

November, 2019
San Diego, California

Dr. Akiko Mikamo
US-Japan Psychological Services
San Diego-WISH: Worldwide Initiative to Safeguard Humanity

APPENDIX A

Photos and Maps

(Use or copying of any graphics without permission is strictly prohibited.)

8:15

Shinji's parents: father and birth mother.
(Photograph by Unknown/Owned by Shinji Mikamo)

Shinji in Kokumin-Fuku (National uniform required for Japanese males during 1940-1945) when he was about 16 years old. (Photograph by Shinji's father/Owned by Shinji Mikamo)

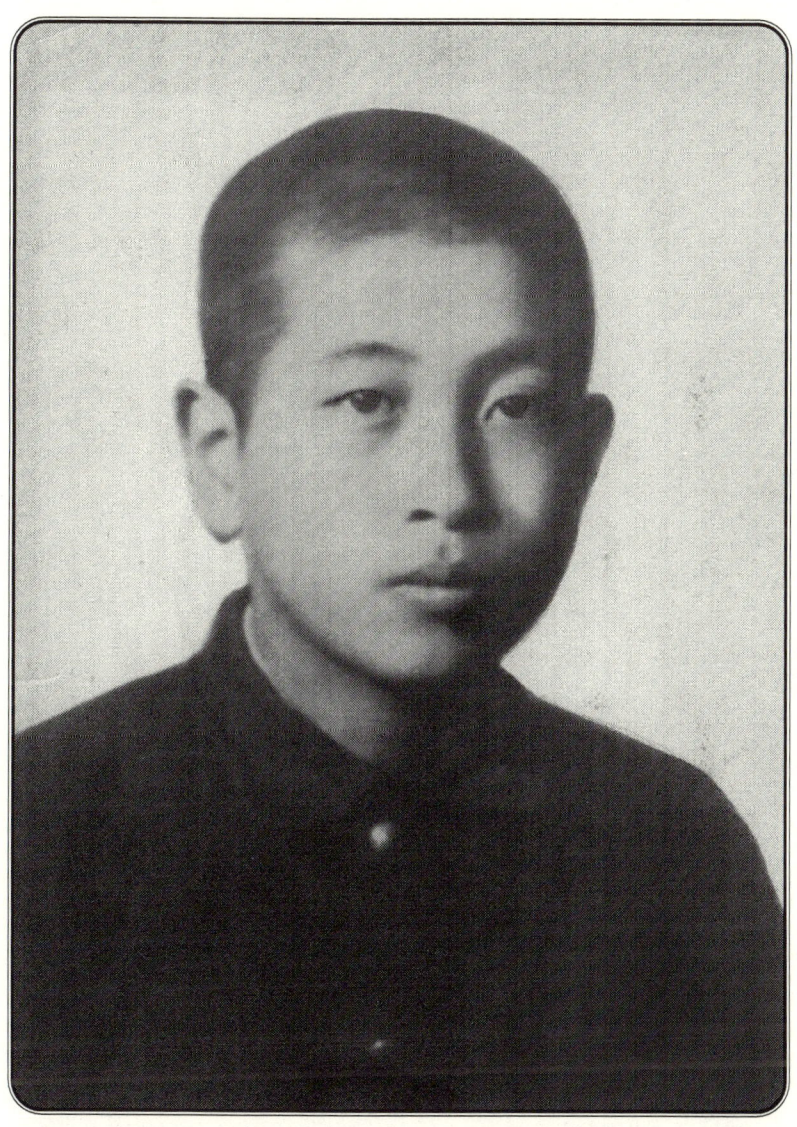

8:15

Shinji's brother, Takaji, in his school uniform when he was 18 years old. (Photograph by Shinji's father/Owned by Shinji Mikamo)

The house key and medal that were chained to Shinji's father's pocket watch. (Photograph by Shinji Mikamo)

8:15

Miyoko's family before the Atomic Bombing (Front: mother, younger sister, father, youngest brother. Back: oldest brother, second oldest brother, Miyoko at age 17). (Photograph by Unknown/Owned by Shinji Mikamo)

DR. AKIKO MIKAMO

A-bomb mushroom cloud photographed from U.S. Army airplane, August 6, 1945. (Photograph by the U.S. Army/ Owned by Hiroshima Peace Memorial Museum)

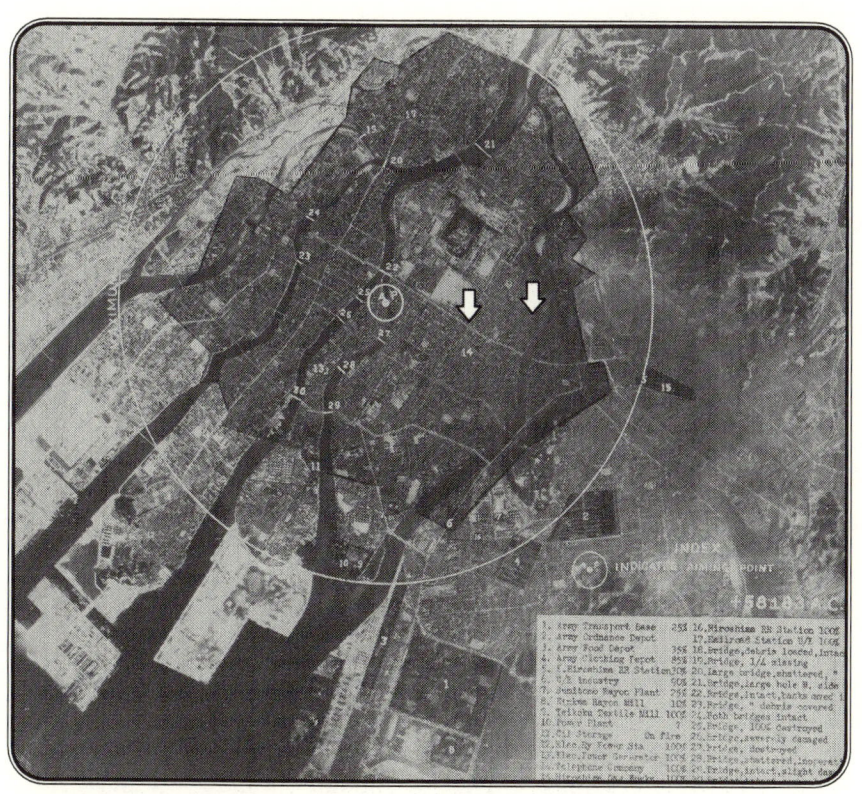

8:15

Aerial view of Hiroshima City with the area marked in dark color for the "100% demolition zone," with the arrows showing Miyoko's location (left) and Shinji's location (right) at the time of bombing. (Provided by U.S. Army Stimson Center/Owned by Hiroshima Peace Memorial Museum)

Shinji's neighborhood and the river he escaped to shortly after the bombing, three quarters of a mile (1,200m) from the epicenter. (Photograph by Toshio Kawamoto, taken at the end of August 1945)

8:15

Shadow of the building (top left) that Miyoko was inside at the time of the bombing, half a mile (800m) from the epicenter. (Photograph by Yotsugi Kawahara/Owned by Hiroshima Peace Memorial Museum, taken September 1945)

Shinji's Footsteps, The first 3 Days

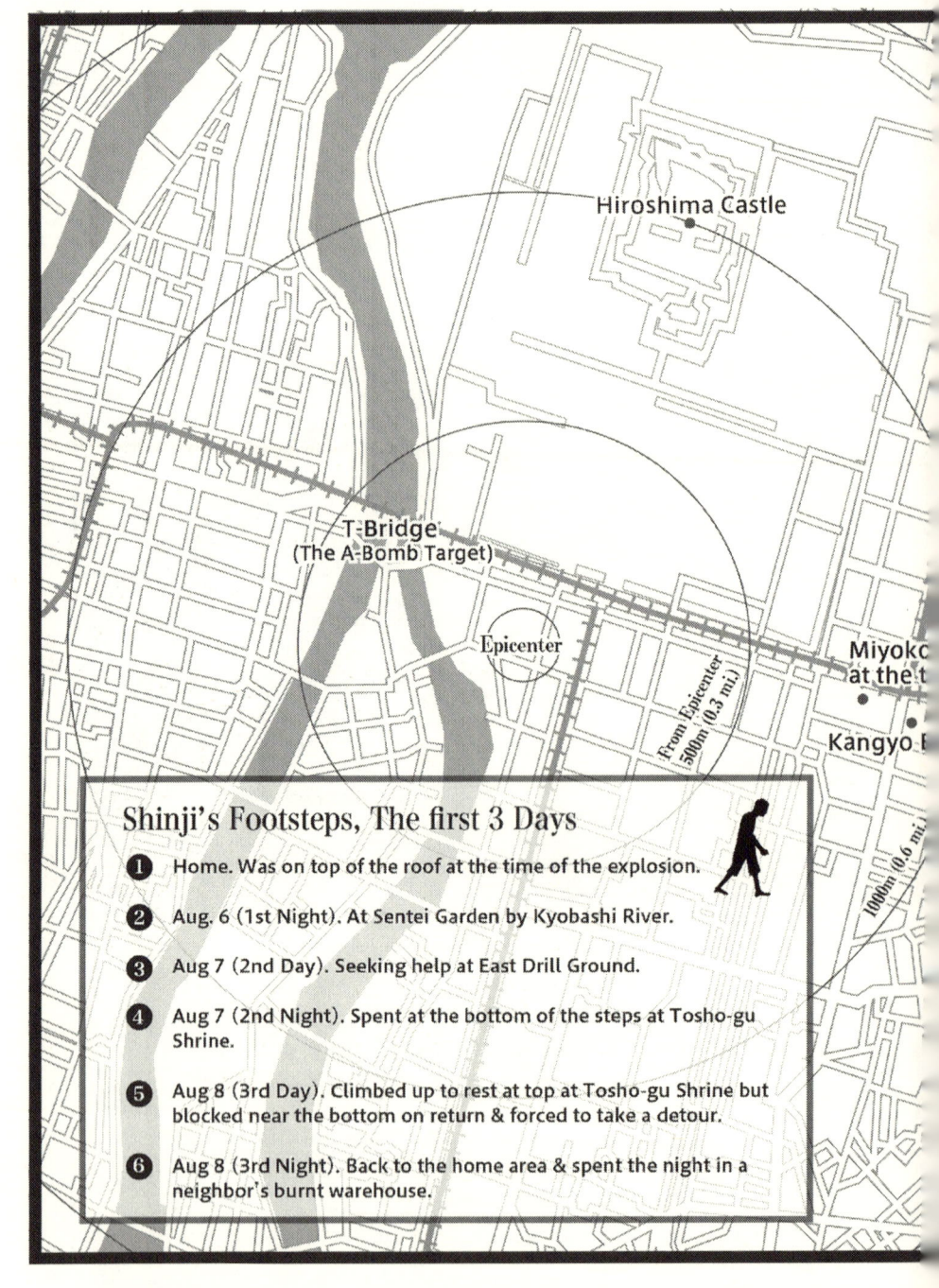

1. Home. Was on top of the roof at the time of the explosion.
2. Aug. 6 (1st Night). At Sentei Garden by Kyobashi River.
3. Aug 7 (2nd Day). Seeking help at East Drill Ground.
4. Aug 7 (2nd Night). Spent at the bottom of the steps at Tosho-gu Shrine.
5. Aug 8 (3rd Day). Climbed up to rest at top at Tosho-gu Shrine but blocked near the bottom on return & forced to take a detour.
6. Aug 8 (3rd Night). Back to the home area & spent the night in a neighbor's burnt warehouse.

Map of Hiroshima city showing the proximity and route Shinji and his father took to escape for the first 3 days. (Graphic by Uz Inc.)

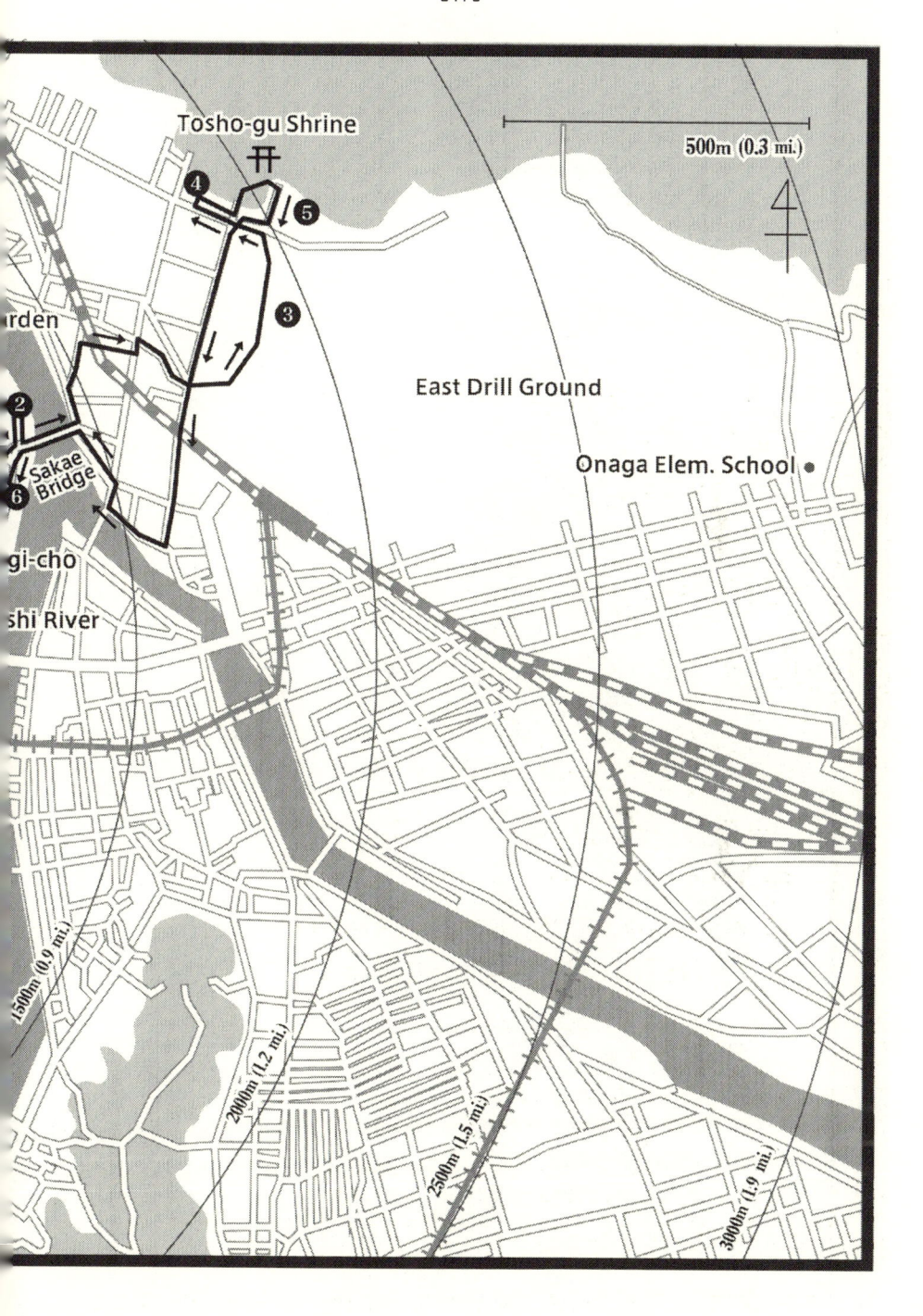

8:15

Tosho-gu Shrine

500m (0.3 mi.)

East Drill Ground

Onaga Elem. School

Sakae Bridge

gi-chō

shi River

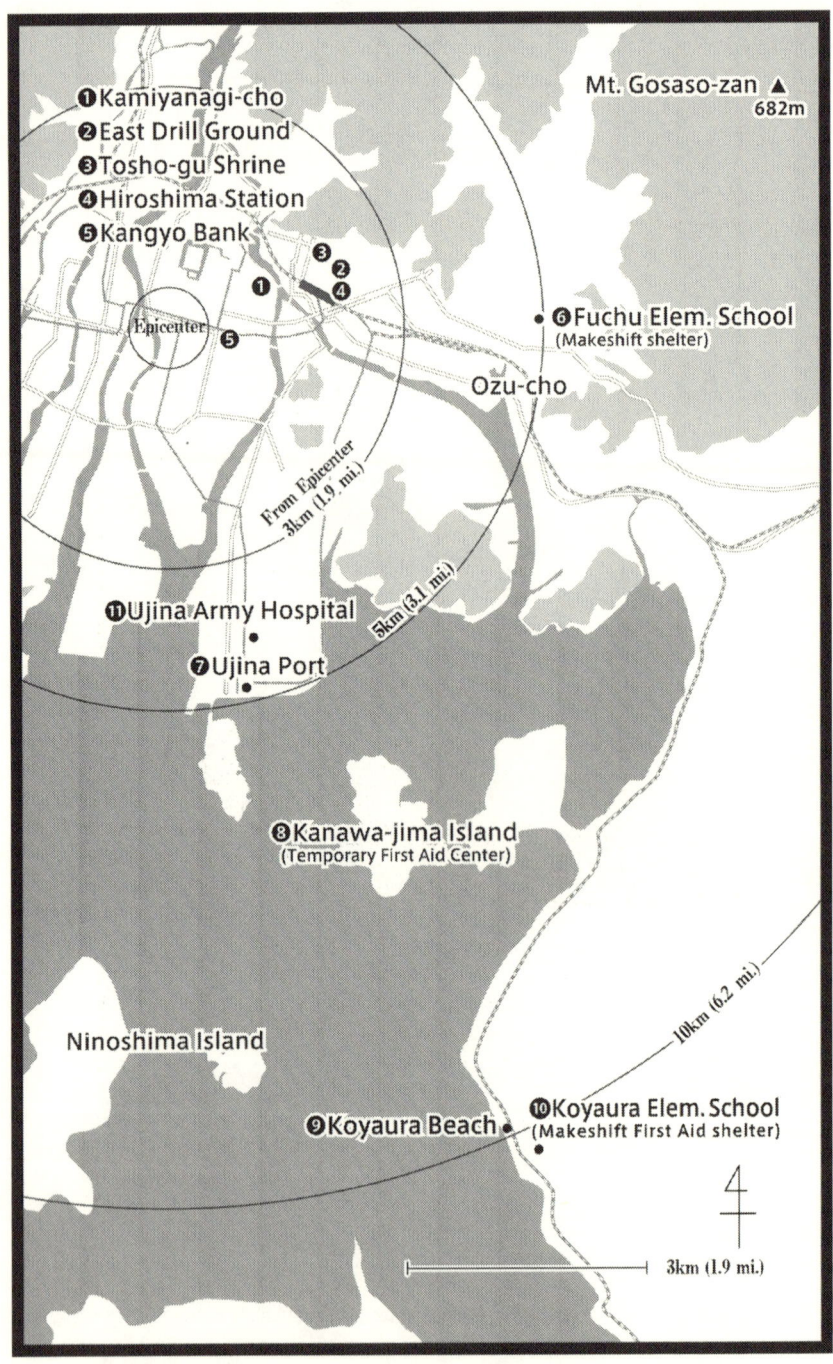

Map of Hiroshima city and surrounding area showing Shinji's footsteps in the first 9 days and beyond. (Graphic by Uz Inc.)

8:15

Shinji's Father's heat-fused pocket watch
(Photograph owned by Hiroshima Peace Memorial Museum)

Shinji & Miyoko after the war.
(Photograph by Unknown/Owned by Shinji Mikamo)

8:15

Miyoko's family after the Atomic Bombing (mother, father, baby Sanae, Miyoko, aunt, youngest brother, Shinji). (Photograph by Unknown/Owned by Shinji Mikamo)

Sakae Bridge & Kyobashi River today. (Photograph by Andrew J. Flores)

8:15

Tosho-gu Shrine Today (Photography by Rie Nii)

Peace Memorial Park and the Atomic Bomb Dome today.
(Photograph by Andrew J. Flores)

8:15

Another World Cultural Heritage site, the Torii Gate of Miyajima in Hiroshima Prefecture, one of the three most scenic sites in Japan. (Photograph by Andrew J. Flores)

Shinji at 87 years old.
(Photograph by Andrew J. Flores, Shinji's grandson)

APPENDIX B

President Barack Obama's Hiroshima Speech

May 27, 2016

SEVENTY-ONE YEARS AGO, ON a bright cloudless morning, death fell from the sky and the world was changed. A flash of light and a wall of fire destroyed a city and demonstrated that mankind possessed the means to destroy itself.

Why do we come to this place, to Hiroshima? We come to ponder a terrible force unleashed in a not-so-distant past. We come to mourn the dead, including over 100,000 Japanese men, women and children, thousands of Koreans, a dozen Americans held prisoner.

Their souls speak to us. They ask us to look inward, to take stock of who we are and what we might become.

It is not the fact of war that sets Hiroshima apart. Artifacts tell us that violent conflict appeared with the very first man. Our early ancestors having learned to make blades from flint and spears from wood used these tools not just for hunting but against their own kind. On every continent, the history of civilization is filled with war, whether driven by scarcity of grain or hunger for gold, compelled by nationalist fervor or religious zeal. Empires have risen and fallen. Peoples have been subjugated and liberated. And at each juncture, innocents have suffered, a countless toll, their names forgotten by time.

The world war that reached its brutal end in Hiroshima and Nagasaki was fought among the wealthiest and most powerful of nations. Their civilizations had given the world great cities and magnificent art. Their thinkers had advanced ideas of justice and harmony and truth. And yet the war grew out of the same base instinct for domination or conquest that had caused conflicts among the simplest tribes, an old pattern amplified by new capabilities and without new constraints.

In the span of a few years, some 60 million people would die. Men, women, children, no different than us. Shot, beaten, marched, bombed, jailed, starved, gassed to death. There are many sites around the world that chronicle this war, memorials that tell stories of courage and heroism, graves and empty camps that echo of unspeakable depravity.

Yet in the image of a mushroom cloud that rose into these skies, we are most starkly reminded of humanity's core contradiction. How the very spark that marks us as a species, our thoughts, our imagination, our language, our toolmaking, our ability to set ourselves apart from nature and bend it to our will — those very things also give us the capacity for unmatched destruction. How often does material advancement or social innovation blind us to this truth? How easily we learn to justify violence in the name of some higher cause.

Every great religion promises a pathway to love and peace and righteousness, and yet no religion has been spared from believers who have claimed their faith as a license to kill.

Nations arise telling a story that binds people together in sacrifice and cooperation, allowing for remarkable feats. But those same stories have so often been used to oppress and dehumanize those who are different.

Science allows us to communicate across the seas and fly above the clouds, to cure disease and understand the cosmos, but those same discoveries can be turned into ever more efficient killing machines.

The wars of the modern age teach us this truth. Hiroshima teaches this truth. Technological progress without an equivalent progress in human institutions can doom us. The scientific revolution that led to the splitting of an atom requires a moral revolution as well.

That is why we come to this place. We stand here in the middle of this city and force ourselves to imagine the moment the bomb fell. We force ourselves to feel the dread of children confused by what they see. We listen to a silent cry. We remember all the innocents killed across the arc of that terrible war and the wars that came before and the wars that would follow.

Mere words cannot give voice to such suffering. But we have a shared responsibility to look directly into the eye of history and ask what we must do differently to curb such suffering again.

Some day, the voices of the hibakusha will no longer be with us to bear witness. But the memory of the morning of Aug. 6, 1945, must never fade. That memory allows us to fight complacency. It fuels our moral imagination. It allows us to change.

And since that fateful day, we have made choices that give us hope. The United States and Japan have forged not only an alliance but a friendship that has won far more for our people than we could ever claim through war. The nations of Europe built a union that replaced battlefields with bonds of commerce and democracy. Oppressed people and nations won liberation. An international community established institutions and treaties that work to avoid war and aspire to restrict and roll back and ultimately eliminate the existence of nuclear weapons.

Still, every act of aggression between nations, every act of terror and corruption and cruelty and oppression that we see around the world shows our work is never done. We may not be able to eliminate man's capacity to do evil, so nations and the alliances that we form must possess the means to defend ourselves. But among those nations like my own that hold nuclear stockpiles, we must have the courage to escape the logic of fear and pursue a world without them.

We may not realize this goal in my lifetime, but persistent effort can roll back the possibility of catastrophe. We can chart a course that leads to the destruction of these stockpiles. We can stop the spread to new nations and secure deadly materials from fanatics.

And yet that is not enough. For we see around the world today how even the crudest rifles and barrel bombs can serve up violence on a terrible scale. We must change our mind-set about war itself. To prevent conflict through diplomacy and strive to end conflicts after they've begun. To see our growing interdependence as a cause for peaceful cooperation and not violent competition. To define our nations not by our capacity to destroy but by what we build. And perhaps, above all, we must re-imagine our connection to one another as members of one human race.

For this, too, is what makes our species unique. We're not bound by genetic code to repeat the mistakes of the past. We can learn. We can choose. We can tell our children a different story, one that describes a common humanity, one that makes war less likely and cruelty less easily accepted.

We see these stories in the hibakusha. The woman who forgave a pilot who flew the plane that dropped the atomic bomb because she recognized that what she really hated was war itself. The man who sought out families of Americans killed here because he believed their loss was equal to his own.

My own nation's story began with simple words: All men are created equal and endowed by our creator with certain unalienable rights including life, liberty and the pursuit of happiness. Realizing that ideal has never been easy, even within our own borders, even among our own citizens. But staying true to that story is worth the effort. It is an ideal to be strived for, an ideal that extends across continents and across oceans. The irreducible worth of every person, the insistence that every life is precious, the radical and necessary notion that we are part of a single human family — that is the story that we all must tell.

That is why we come to Hiroshima. So that we might think of people we love. The first smile from our children in the morning. The gentle touch from a spouse over the kitchen table. The comforting embrace of a parent. We can think of those things and know that those same precious moments took place here, 71 years ago.

Those who died, they are like us. Ordinary people understand this, I think. They do not want more war. They would rather that the wonders of science be focused on improving life and not eliminating it. When the choices made by nations, when the choices made by leaders, reflect this simple wisdom, then the lesson of Hiroshima is done.

The world was forever changed here, but today the children of this city will go through their day in peace. What a precious thing that is. It is worth protecting, and then extending to every child. That is a future we can choose, a future in which Hiroshima and Nagasaki are known not as the dawn of atomic warfare but as the start of our own moral awakening.

ABOUT THE AUTHOR

Dr. Mikamo was born and raised in Hiroshima by two atomic bomb survivors and promised herself as a child to contribute to world peace and humanity, inspired by her father, Shinji Mikamo. She graduated from Hiroshima University, School of Education, and moved to the United States. She obtained Doctor of Psychology in clinical psychology from California School of Professional Psychology, San Diego, Executive Master in Consulting and Coaching for Change from INSEAD in Fontainebleau, France, and Postdoctoral Master of Science in Clinical Psychopharmacology from Alliant International University in San Francisco, California, among other advanced degrees. She is a board certified executive coach, licensed clinical psychologist in California, and licensed medical psychologist with a prescription privilege in Louisiana.

Dr. Mikamo is president of US-Japan Psychological Services (www.usjapanpsych.com), president of San Diego-WISH: Worldwide Initiative to Safeguard Humanity (www.sdwish.org), and Co-Founder of Possibility School (www.possibilityschool.org). She believes that world peace and harmony start with healthy individual psyche and harmonious interpersonal relationships, based on love, tolerance, empathy, forgiveness, and growth mindset. From this perspective, Dr. Mikamo provides executive assessment and coaching, multicultural organizational consultation, psychotherapy, psychological assessment, psychiatric medication consultation, emotional and interpersonal wellness workshops and seminars, inspirations through her writing and speaking, and has taught clinical and educational psychology at various graduate schools.

Furthermore, San Diego-WISH, a not-for-profit 501(3)(c) organization, holds "International Peace & Humanity Day" events on the anniversary of the Hiroshima and Nagasaki bombings to educate the global communities and young generations to promote world peace and for the betterment of humanity.

In 2014, Dr. Mikamo received *Award for Exceptional Services to Humanity* from World Peace and Prosperity Foundation at House of Lords in Westminster Palace, in London, United Kingdom, for her work to send the messages of forgiveness and resilience to the world.

Made in the USA
Middletown, DE
05 May 2023